ISLES OF SCILLY

Isles of Scilly

RCC PILOTAGE FOUNDATION

Graham Adam

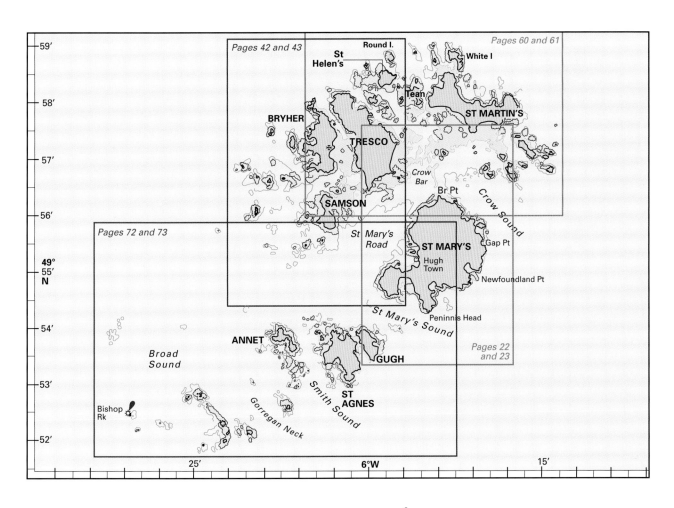

Imray Laurie Norie & Wilson

Published by
Imray Laurie Norie & Wilson Ltd
Wych House The Broadway
St Ives Cambridgeshire PE27 5BT England
www.imray.com
2010

© Text: Royal Cruising Club Pilotage Foundation
2010
© Photographs: Graham Adam, except where stated
© Aerial photographs: Patrick Roach
© Plans: Imray Laurie Norie & Wilson Ltd
1994, 2010

The plans and tidal information have been
reproduced with the permission of the
Hydrographic Office of the United Kingdom
(Licence No. HO151/951101/01) and the controller
of Her Britannic Majesty's Stationery Office.

South England Pilot Volume V Isles of Scilly
    Lt. Col. R. J. Brandon
1st edition 1980
2nd edition 1983

Isles of Scilly Pilot
3rd edition 1994

Isles of Scilly
    Royal Cruising Club Pilotage Foundation
4th edition 1999
5th edition 2010

ISBN 978 085288 850 6

British Library Cataloguing in Publication Data.
A catalogue record for this title is available from the
British Library.

This work, based on surveys over a period of many
years, has been corrected to Ocober 2009 from land-
based visits to the ports and harbours of the coast,
from contributions by visiting yachtsmen and from
official notices. The majority of the aerial photographs
were taken during August 2007

Printed in Singapore by Star Standard Industries Pte

CORRECTIONAL SUPPLEMENTS

This pilot book may be amended at intervals by the
issue of correctional supplements. These are
published on the internet at our web site
www.imray.com (and also via www.rccpf.org.uk)
and may be downloaded free of charge. Printed
copies are also available on request from the
publishers at the above address. Like this pilot,
supplements are selective. Navigators requiring the
latest definitive information are advised to refer to
official hydrographic office data.

ADDITIONAL INFORMATION

Additional information may be found under the
Publications page at www.rccpf.org.uk. This
includes a downloadable waypoint list, links to
Google maps, additional photographs and mid
season updates when appropriate. Passage
planning information may also be found on that
website.

CAUTION

Whilst the RCC Pilotage Foundation, the author and the publishers have
used reasonable endeavours to ensure the accuracy of the content of this
book, it contains selected information and thus is not definitive. It does
not contain all known information on the subject in hand and should not
be relied on alone for navigational use: it should only be used in
conjunction with official hydrographic data. This is particularly relevant
to the plans, which should not be used for navigation.

The RCC Pilotage Foundation, the author and the publishers believe that
the information which they have included is a useful aid to prudent
navigation, but the safety of a vessel depends ultimately on the judgment
of the skipper, who should assess all information, published or
unpublished.

The information provided in this pilot book may be out of date and may
be changed or updated without notice. The RCC Pilotage Foundation
cannot accept any liability for any error, omission or failure to update
such information.

To the extent permitted by law, the RCC Pilotage Foundation, the
author(s) and the publishers do not accept liability for any loss and/or
damage howsoever caused that may arise from reliance on information
contained in these pages.

POSITIONS

All positions in the text are to WGS 84 datum. They are supplied as aids
to help orientation and to assist in locating and maintaining transits
referred to in the book. As always, care must be exercised to work to the
datum of the chart in use.

WAYPOINTS

This edition of the Isles of Scilly pilot includes the introduction of
waypoints. The RCC Pilotage Foundation consider a waypoint to be a
position likely to be helpful for navigation if entered into some form of
electronic navigation system for use in conjunction with GPS. In this
pilot they have been derived from current Admiralty charts. They must
be used with caution. All waypoints are given to datum WGS 84 and
every effort has been made to ensure their accuracy. Nevertheless, for
each individual vessel, the standard of onboard equipment, aerial
position, datum setting, correct entry of data and operator skill all play a
part in their effectiveness. In particular it is vital for the navigator to note
the datum of the chart in use and apply the necessary correction if
plotting a GPS position on the chart.

Our use of the term 'waypoint' does not imply that all vessels can safely
sail directly over those positions at all times. Some – as in this pilot – may
be linked to indicate recommended routes under appropriate conditions.
However, skippers should be aware of the risk of collision with another
vessel, which is plying the exact reciprocal course. Verification by
observation, or use of radar to check the accuracy of a waypoint, may
sometimes be advisable and reassuring.

We emphasise that we regard waypoints as an aid to navigation for use
as the navigator or skipper decides. We hope that the waypoints in this
pilot will help ease that navigational load.

PLANS

The plans in this guide are not to be used for navigation – they are
designed to support the text and should always be used together with
navigational charts. Waypoints should not be selected using the latitude
and longitude scales of these plans.

It should be borne in mind that the characteristics of lights may be
changed during the life of the book, and that in any case notification of
such changes is unlikely to be reported immediately. Each light is
identified in both the text and where possible on the plans (where it
appears in magenta) by its international index number, as used in the
Admiralty List of Lights, from which the book may be updated.

All bearings are given from seaward and refer to true north. Symbols are
based on those used by the British Admiralty – users are referred to
Symbols and Abbreviations (NP 5011).

CONTENTS

THE RCC PILOTAGE FOUNDATION

In 1976 an American member of the Royal Cruising Club, Dr Fred Ellis, indicated that he wished to make a gift to the Club in memory of his father, the late Robert E. Ellis, of his friends Peter Pye and John Ives and as a mark of esteem for Roger Pinckney. An independent charity known as the RCC Pilotage Foundation was formed and Dr Ellis added his house to his already generous gift of money to form the Foundation's permanent endowment. The Foundation's charitable objective is 'to advance the education of the public in the science and practice of navigation' which is at present achieved through the writing and updating of pilot books covering many different parts of the world.

The Foundation is extremely grateful and privileged to have been given the copyrights to books written by a number of distinguished authors and yachtsmen including the late Adlard Coles, Robin Brandon and Malcolm Robson. In return the Foundation has willingly accepted the task of keeping the original books up to date and many yachtsmen and women have helped (and are helping) the Foundation fulfill this commitment. In addition to the titles donated to the Foundation, several new books have been created and developed under the auspices of the Foundation. The Foundation works in close collaboration with three publishers – Imray Laurie Norie and Wilson, Adlard Coles Nautical and On Board Publications – and in addition publishes in its own name short run guides and pilot books for areas where limited demand does not justify large print runs. Several of the Foundation's books have been translated into French, German and Italian.

The Foundation runs its own website at www.rccpf.org.uk which not only lists all the publications but also contains free downloadable pilotage information.

The overall management of the Foundation is entrusted to trustees appointed by the Royal Cruising Club, with day to day operations being controlled by the Director. All these appointments are unpaid. In line with its charitable status, the Foundation distributes no profits, these are used to finance new books and developments and to subsidise publications covering areas of low demand.

PUBLICATIONS OF THE RCC PILOTAGE FOUNDATION

Imray
Faroe, Iceland and
 Greenland
Norway
The Baltic Sea
Channel Islands
North Brittany and
 the Channel Islands
Isles of Scilly
North Biscay
South Biscay
Atlantic Islands
Atlantic Spain & Portugal
Mediterranean Spain:
 Costas del Sol and Blanca
 Costas del Azahar,
  Dorada & Brava
Islas Baleares
Corsica and North Sardinia
Chile
North Africa

Adlard Coles Nautical
Atlantic Crossing Guide
Pacific Crossing Guide

On Board Publications
South Atlantic Circuit
Havens and Anchorages
 for the South American
 Coast

**The RCC Pilotage
Foundation**
Supplement to Falkland
 Island Shores
Guide to West Africa
Argentina

**RCCPF Website
www.rccpf.org.uk**
Supplements
Support files for books
Passage Planning Guides
Web Pilots

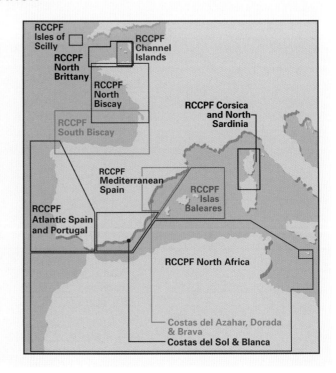

FOREWORD

The origins of this book go back to 1980 and Robin Brandon's *South England Pilot Volume V* which was subsequently revised for the Royal Cruising Club Pilotage Foundation by John and Fay Garey. Graham Adam has now built upon this earlier skilful work to produce this new book. It is aimed at all yachtsmen who wish to visit and enjoy these magnificent islands.

The Isles of Scilly form a compact but complicated group which, with rapid changes of weather and tide, can pose a major challenge to sailors. This is an area where the use of transits and day marks has guided seamen for centuries. In this edition we have introduced waypoints to help approaching navigators to identify transits safely. However, whilst electronic navigation aids may greatly assist with navigation this is an area which demands continuous visual alertness and full use of the long established fixed reference points – this book has been structured accordingly.

The Pilotage Foundation is grateful to Graham Adam for his very detailed recce of these islands together with close liaison with local island experts and for compiling this edition, to his supporters for their additional contributions and photographs, and to Imray for the provision of air photographs by Patrick Roach. As ever, it is Willie Wilson and his team at Imray who have made this publication possible.

Yachtsmen are asked to help those who follow in their wake by alerting the Pilotage Foundation to any changes they may find both in the Isles of Scilly or elsewhere in the areas covered by our publications. Full details of these and our Passage Planning Guides may be found on www.rccpf.org.uk.

Martin Walker
Hon Director
RCC Pilotage Foundation
January 2010

Acknowledgements

The editors wish to thank the people of Scilly and others for their considerable assistance in the preparation of this updated edition. In particular they are grateful to Hamish Anderson and Linda Le Page, Dan Bennett, Henry Birch, Captain Glen Covell and his staff, Captain Peter Crawford, Robert Dorrien-Smith, Susie & Mark Groves, Mike Lewin-Harris, Bryony & Nick Lishman, David Lomax, Peter Martin, Peter Odling-Smee, Ian Sibley, Dick Trafford, Jane Trahair and members of the Boatmen's Association.

Watermill Cove, St Mary's
Patrick Roach

Tean Sound, St Martin's *Patrick Roach*

1. INTRODUCTION

Scilly lies about 28 miles from Land's End. This is not a great distance from the mainland and indeed Land's End can easily be seen from Scilly in clear weather. But the islands are out in the ocean and, to this day, many 'mainlanders' do not know of the existence of this beautiful archipelago. The Isles of Scilly are made up of over 50 islands and hundreds of drying rocks although only five are inhabited permanently and one more, Gugh, has just two holiday houses. There is often confusion because of duplication in the names of islands, rocks, villages and bays; there are, for example, no less than twelve rocks named 'Round Rock', five named Biggal and four called 'Tearing Ledge'. Local terminology needs some explanation, in particular two widely used words; 'Porth' means bay and 'Carn' correlates with Cairn or Tor. It is about nine and a half miles from the Bishop Rock Light, at the SW extremity of Scilly to the N of White Island at the NE of the isles and about five miles across from the outer limit of the Norrard Rocks to the south coast of St Mary's. The total 'year round' population of Scilly is little over 2,000, the vast majority living on St Mary's, but the numbers are swelled by the many visitors, particularly in the summer season.

There has been human life on the islands for at least 4,000 years evidenced by the many burial chambers from the pre-bronze age period. The inhabitants of the islands now make their living primarily from tourism but horticulture, fishing and crafts still play their part. In the past fishing, boat building, kelping and, most famously, pilotage and salvage all featured at different times in the islands' history. Two themes have been fairly constant. The first has been an intimate relationship with the sea; to this day the seamen of Scilly are renowned for their courage and seamanship. The second is the need for initiative and resourcefulness to cope in an environment where sourcing materials and expertise is not as straightforward as it might be on the mainland.

Until early in the 20th century even the tax man was not prepared to force his attentions on the inhabitants. From Redruth in Cornwall income tax was assessed on Scilly dwellers but no effort was made to enforce collection. If, before the arrival of air transport, the tax man did not wish to attempt the passage to Scilly by boat, he was probably also influenced by the lack of protected harbours when he did arrive.

Most UK-registered yachts arrive in the Isles of Scilly from nearby home ports in Cornwall or Devon, their owners making their annual

Scillonian III arriving at the busy quay, St Mary's
David Lomax

pilgrimage to their favourite offshore islands. Perhaps the lack of British yachts from further afield is due to the substantial distance to Scilly from major yachting centres, limitations on time available for the return passage and the difficulty in finding a suitable weather window. Those who persevere with the trip to Scilly, however, will be rewarded by some of the most beautiful scenery in all England, together with bird-life and flowers of an unrivalled nature.

In recent years there has been an abundance of foreign yachts and French-flag vessels now account for about sixty per cent of all arrivals in the islands, outnumbering even the British yachts. The next largest group of visiting yachts come from Ireland followed by Dutch, German and Belgian flags which appear in about equal numbers. The busiest time of the year is from the beginning of June to the end of September with a peak in July and August but it is a long period of settled weather which brings the largest influx of yachts and in a poor summer the numbers fall away noticeably. For many of the foreign-flag vessels, Scilly is a staging post on the way to more distant destinations. For example, many French yachts are bound for southern Ireland and, conversely Irish yachts are bound for Brittany.

An outboard motor casing put to good use!

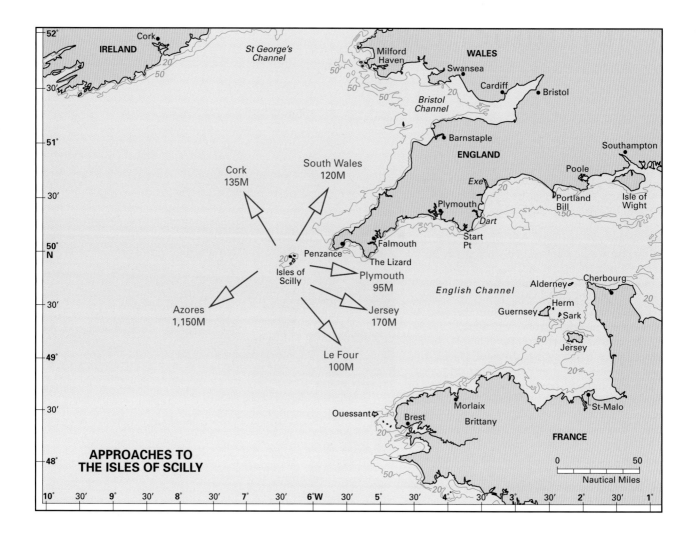

APPROACHES TO
THE ISLES OF SCILLY

Scilly is accessible from Ireland, Wales, The Channel Islands and France as well as the Cornish mainland

Scilly is not a suitable area for the inexperienced yachtsman. The approach can be affected by severe weather with little advance warning and there can also be a sudden reduction in visibility. There are strong and sometimes unpredictable tidal streams in the offing and many tricky unmarked dangers. In recent years the buoyage has been greatly improved and many navigation marks are now lit but the number of rocks and shoal waters make the area unsuitable for navigation at night except for those with local knowledge. No anchorage offers 100% protection from wind and sea, and when the wind changes it may be necessary to move elsewhere in difficult conditions. Scilly, however, presents no more difficulties than many other destinations around Britain. A well-found yacht is necessary, together with up-to-date charts of the area and approaches, and appropriate navigational aids and publications. An auxiliary engine in good working order is a must. Otherwise, the essential factor is a careful study beforehand of the approaches both from charts and from photographs, together with accurate note-taking about tidal streams, tide times and heights as well as the daymarks and lights likely to be met in the approaches. Scilly is just the place to test your abilities in demanding, yet beautiful surroundings.

Most sailing vessels visiting Scilly are fin-keel yachts, although there is a fair assortment of bilge-keelers, catamarans and trimarans. These shallow draft vessels, together with enterprising fin-keelers who have brought legs, are able to enjoy some of the many shallow harbours and bays. This guide examines in some detail the all-tide anchorages where a yacht drawing around 1.8m may always lie afloat and where space exists for more than four or five vessels. There are some other all-tide anchorages which are given consideration. These anchorages suffer from certain disadvantages; for example they may offer little or no shelter from more than moderate sea or wind or they have only limited room for a few yachts.

This guide also includes a selection of other anchorages. Many of these are little more than small coves which skilled yachtsmen may wish to enter in shoal-draught craft in settled weather despite disadvantages such as lack of tidal depth, dubious holding or poor shelter in bad weather.

In addition to anchorages and their facilities, some notes on the islands' history are included, together with some facts about the birds, animals and flowers to be found in this Atlantic Arcadia.

Pilotage in the Isles of Scilly

It is best to arrange the final approach to Scilly so as to allow enough time to anchor in daylight. All other arrangements and plans for making a visit to Scilly should be made with this in mind. Because the islands are so low (with no land higher than 46 metres) the recognition of visual marks is especially important. For this reason navigators should carry, and be prepared to use, an accurate hand-bearing compass, a good pair of binoculars and up-to-date large-scale charts. With such basic equipment, competent navigators can manage without electronic aids when sailing in and around Scilly, although most sailors will find a depth gauge, radar, and GPS or a chart plotter to be helpful when approaching and cruising around the islands.

The Isles of Scilly are in effect a plateau and, when clear of the islands, the depths are universally in excess of 50m. In poor visibility a reliable depth sounder is a useful navigational tool. It should be noted however that once the 50m contour is crossed the seabed can rise steeply to dangerously shoal depths.

The seamen of Scilly have themselves long used daymarks and transits for navigation and, in conditions where strong winds and tides often prevail, such immovable objects are reliable navigational tools. Careful observation not only enables one to check position fixes obtained electronically, but also aids recognition of and familiarity with the geography, both of which are fundamental to safe pilotage.

There is a lot of shoal water among the islands, and submerged rocks and sandbanks are everywhere. Fortunately, the area is well charted but many of the hazards are not marked by buoys or beacons and may only be visible at LW. The golden rule when sailing among the islands is to do so on a flood tide, ideally after half tide. Individual yachtsmen, however, must make their own assessment of conditions as barometric pressure, among other factors, can have a great affect on sea level.

Another point to bear in mind when navigating among these islands is: 'never follow the ferries'. Despite their size (some are over 20 metres long) they are all very shallow-draught, the boatmen know the waters intimately and they are accustomed to skimming over sandbanks with just enough water beneath their keel.

Transits and bearings of reference

Transits are widely used in this guide and the importance of steering to offset leeway and tidal streams when using transits cannot be overemphasised. Never leave an inexperienced person on the helm to look over their shoulder at a stern transit in a strong cross tide! In Scilly they will soon find the bottom.

A rare treat – at anchor off the Western Rocks on a calm day
Mike Lewin-Harris

Rocks off Annet Head

Swell across the entrance to Old Grimsby Sound between Tresco and Golden Ball

The importance of arriving in Scilly in daylight has already been highlighted, and it should be equally stressed that a passage to these islands should never be attempted in bad weather. Yachts lying snugly in mainland harbours should stay where they are if fog or gales are forecast. If already en route to the islands, one should not try to enter them in gale conditions. Strong winds from any direction, superimposed on the almost everlasting swell from the Atlantic, are a recipe for trouble in the narrow, tidal, rocky sounds.

Waypoints

Waypoints have been provided in this pilot as an aid to navigation. They have been positioned primarily to allow navigators to approach safely to the islands and the prime transits, and to aid recognition and maintenance on and along a transit. They are selected to assist with visual navigation and must not be used as a substitute for it.

Other Pilotage considerations

Swells from the Atlantic, are a recipe for trouble in the narrow, tidal, rocky, sounds. Gales or strong winds from the southwest, for example, will not mean that calm waters will be found to the north of the islands; the swell will sweep around the Scillies and make any approach from the north highly dangerous.

Remember too that the islands are low and largely cliffless, and therefore radar echoes will not give a clear image of the shore (let alone of the off-lying rocks). In poor visibility (particularly fog) it is wise to stand off clear of the shipping lanes and await clearer conditions.

If caught out by a gale en route, the following courses of action are open, depending on the direction of the wind:

1. Heave-to clear of the shipping lanes, in particular the Traffic Separation zones, and await better weather.

2. Proceed to Mounts Bay and take shelter in Newlyn or Penzance. (Note that the dock gate in Penzance Inner Harbour entrance only opens between HW -2h and HW +1h. Six yellow holding buoys are laid in season S of the lighthouse pier for waiting yachts which should call the harbourmaster on VHF Ch.12 to notify their intention to enter.

3. Proceed to St Ives Bay and anchor.

4. Proceed to Cork harbour in SE Ireland.

Measurements, bearings, distances and charts

Distances are given in sea miles (M) and occasionally in metres and decimetres. Soundings and drying heights are given in metres at Lowest Astronomical Tide (LAT) and elevations (in metres) are given as above the level of Mean High Water Springs (MHWS). Bearings are True and the 360 degree notation is used. Directional safety is shown using cardinal and sub-cardinal points, and bearings and directions are from seaward.

In this publication the charts referred to in connection with pilotage at Scilly are Admiralty charts 34 and 883. These charts should be standard equipment on visiting yachts and it is suggested that readers refer to them while reading this guide. Admiralty charts 1148 and 2565 are also helpful if making the passage from the UK mainland.

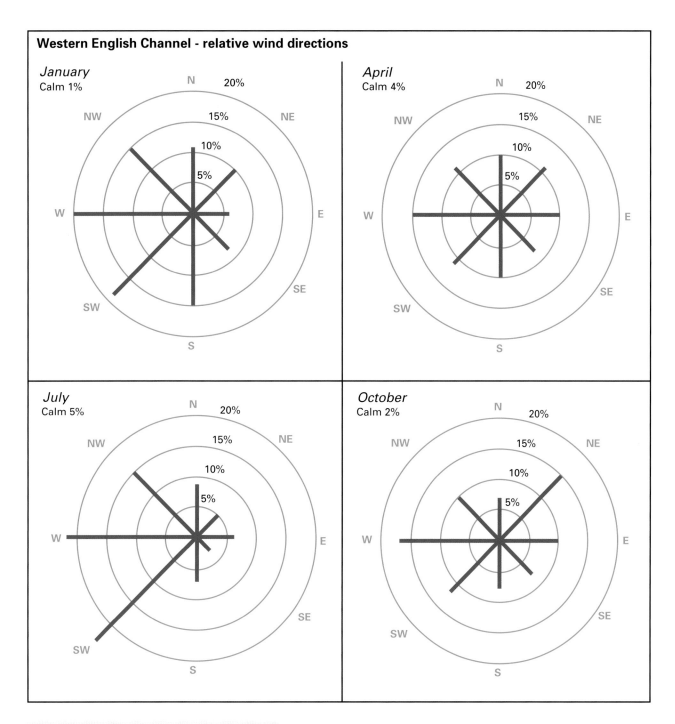

Western English Channel - relative wind directions

Meteorology

The Isles of Scilly have the most unpredictable and rapidly changing weather conditions. The prudent skipper will obtain every forecast available and will keep a radio and visual watch for gale warnings. (See page 9.) A careful watch should also be kept on the barometer for indications of deteriorating weather despite what the weather forecasts predict. In unsettled weather secondary depressions may form to the W of the islands and quickly produce a very rough sea.

Winds

Winds are mainly from the W, with winds from NW, SW and N the next most common. SE winds are the least frequent, as the wind roses show (opposite). Light sea breezes are sometimes a feature during warm fine summer afternoons and weak land breezes may be found at night.

Gales

There are more gales the further W along the S coast of England one proceeds. The average frequency of gales a month is as follows:

Jan	Feb	Mar	Apr	May	Jun
4.7	2.8	2.6	1.4	1.1	0.1

Jul	Aug	Sep	Oct	Nov	Dec
0.4	0.6	1.4	2.3	3.5	5.7

They are usually associated with deep depressions moving within 400M. Wind speeds of 90 knots have been recorded, but this is very exceptional, the usual maximum wind speed being between 34 and 47 knots (Beaufort force 8–9).

Clouds

The average cloud cover is 5 to 6 octas (eighths) throughout the year, showing a slight improvement in the afternoon in the area of the Isles of Scilly.

Precipitation

Snow, hail and sleet are included with rain. There are considerable yearly and monthly variations, which can make nonsense of the averages given below. The greatest amount of rain occurs with the passage of a front and during thunderstorms.

No. of days	Amount 1mm+	mm
January	16·3	95
February	12·4	79
March	12·2	73
April	9·3	48
May	9·7	58
June	8·2	48
July	9·2	54
August	9·6	64
September	11·2	69
October	12·2	82
November	14·7	96
December	15·8	97

Snow

Swell in The Cove, St Agnes

Snow and sleet can fall on the islands at any time between November and April, but the average is 4.4 days a year between January and March. Snow lies 0.5 days a year measured at 0900 hours.

Thunderstorms

Thunderstorms usually form over France at the end of a period of fine weather and drift across the Channel to affect this area.

Fog and visibility

Sea fog can occur at any time when a warm moist air stream crosses a colder mass of water. This usually occurs as a SW–W warm sector air stream approaches this coast; it is most frequent in early summer. Land fog can also occur on cold still nights and days and may drift across the coastline. On the mainland the average is one day of fog a month during the summer months and two to three days a month during the winter. The reverse applies to the area of the Isles of Scilly.

Air temperature

Unusually the average temperature range is only about 10°C. The daily maximum temperature is 19.2°C in August and 9.0°C in February and the average daily minimum temperatures in these months are 13.7°C and 2.6°C, respectively.

Relative humidity

The relative humidity can vary from 100% in rain and fog to about 40% in a dry NE air stream in summer. The average is around 90% at night in winter and around 75% at mid-day in the summer.

Oceanography

Sea surface temperatures

The sea is at its coldest towards the end of February and warmest during August, as follows:

Feb	May	Aug	Nov
9.7°C	11.4°C	16.3°C	12.7°C

Seas

The seas in this area can range from rough (2m) to very high (9m) in strong winds created by deep depressions; they are rarely completely calm.

Swell

The area is subject to swell from the SW-W. During the winter there is a swell of over 4m in height on average 10 days a month.

Sea level

Sea level can depart from predicted tidal levels due to strong winds or unusually high or low barometric pressure. Low pressure of 960mb can raise the sea level by about 0.5m over the predicted level and high pressure of 1040mb can lower the sea level by about 0.3m. Wind-induced surges in the Scilly area are likely to be much smaller than those affecting the coastal areas of the central Irish Sea or eastern England, and are unlikely to exceed 0.5m.

Currents

Currents are created on the surface of the sea by prevailing and recent winds. They run in a direction of about 30° to the right of the wind and their speed is related to the strength of the wind and its duration, being about 1/30th of the wind speed. These currents are most prevalent in winter between November and January, with a frequency of about 9% of the time and a speed of 1 to 2 knots. In summer, from May to July, they only occur for 1% of the time.

Tidal streams (see pages 8–9)

The inshore tidal streams tend to follow the line of the coast, flowing into bays and out at the far end, while offshore streams follow a straighter line up or down channel. When clearing most bays and channels, one must allow for considerable set both into and out of them. In Scilly there are overfalls and tidal eddies which must be allowed for off many points and headlands, while note should be taken that heights, times, speeds and directions of tidal streams around the islands are most irregular. These factors are also affected by the presence of high or low pressure so, even with sophisticated electronic equipment, the best way to cope with the vagaries of tidal streams and currents is to adjust your vessel's course and speed by visual assessment of progress.

Tidal heights

Mean tidal heights are given below.

MHWS	MHWN	ML	MLWS	MLWN
5.7m	4.3m	3.2m	0.7m	2.0m

Chart datum is LAT which is 2.91m below ordnance datum.

To N, W and S of the islands the streams generally run as follows:

Local HW	Plymouth HW	Dover HW	Direction	Rate (knots)	
				Springs	Neaps
−0505	−0600	+0045	WSW–WNW	1.6	0.4
−0205	−0300	+0345	E–ENE	1.6	0.6
+0055	0000	−0540	ENE–ESE	1.3	0.5
+0355	+0300	−0240	S–SW	1.4	0.5
+0555	+0600	+0020	SW–W	1.8	0.5

To the E of the islands and between them and the mainland coast the weakest and strongest streams are:

Local HW	Plymouth HW	Dover HW	Direction	Rate (knots)	
				Springs	Neaps
−0505	−0600	+0045	WNW–NNW	2.2	0.4
−0205	−0300	+0345	NNW–NNE	2.0	0.6
+0055	0000	−0540	E–SE	2.1	0.3
+0355	+0300	−0240	SSE–SSW	2.1	0.7
+0555	+0600	+0020	WSW–NW	1.8	0.4

Note Tidal streams in the various sounds and anchorages are given in the pilotage directions for the particular area.

TIDAL STREAMS (ISLES OF SCILLY)

Note figures refer to mean rates in knots at neaps and springs
thus 03.05 indicates 0.3 knots (neaps) and 0.5 knots (springs)

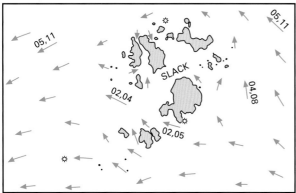

0600 before HW Plymouth
0505 before HW St Mary's

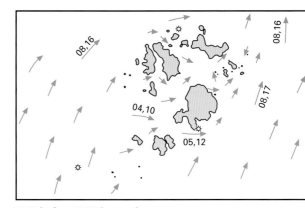

0500 before HW Plymouth
0405 before HW St Mary's

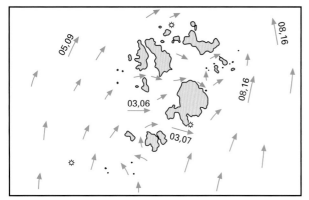

0400 before HW Plymouth
0305 before HW St Mary's

0300 before HW Plymouth
0205 before HW St Mary's

0200 before HW Plymouth
0105 before HW St Mary's

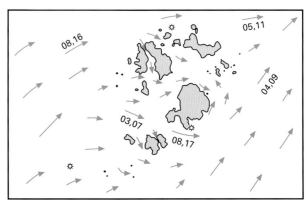

0100 before HW Plymouth
0005 before HW St Mary's

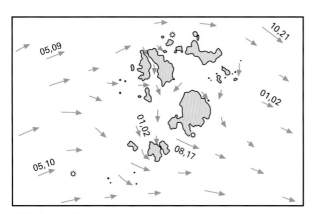

HW Plymouth
0055 after HW St Mary's

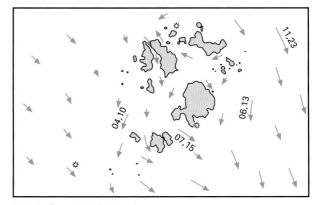

0100 before HW Plymouth
0105 after HW St Mary's

0200 after Plymouth
0255 after HW St Mary's

0300 after HW Plymouth
0355 after HW St Mary's

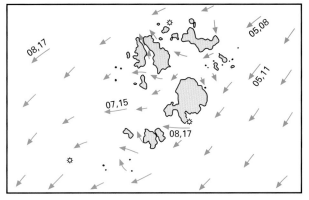

0400 after HW Plymouth
0455 after HW St Mary's

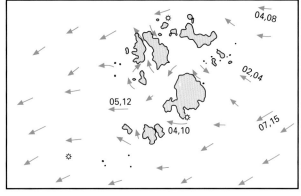

0500 after HW Plymouth
0555 after HW St Mary's

Communications and radio aids

Air radiobeacons

Penzance 333kHz *PH* 15M 50°07'.67N
05°31'W. Sunrise to sunset.
St Mary's, Isles of Scilly 321kHz *STM* 15M
49°54'.82N 06°17'.43W. Sunrise to sunset.

Racons

There are three useful racons in the approaches
to the Isles of Scilly:

Bishop Rock Light	T	18M
Seven Stones light float	O	15M
Wolf Rock	T	10M
Round Island light	M	10M

Radio weather services

Full details of the many radio weather services
available may be found in *RYA Weather Forecasts*.
The following is a selection.

BBC Radio 4

198kHz (1515m) and FM 92.4-94.6mHz.
    All times UT.
0048 Every day, 24-hour, long-range and
        inshore waters forecasts.

0520 Mon-Sat, 24-hour, long-range and
        inshore waters forecasts.
1201 Every day, gale warnings, synopsis and
        24hr forecast. (LW 198kHz only)
1754 Every day, gale warnings, synopsis and
        24hr forecast. (FM weekends only)

BBC Radio Cornwall

96mHz from St Mary's. All times LT.
Full shipping forecast
        Mon – Fri 0645 and 1745
        Sat and Sun – 0745
Inshore waters forecast
        Mon – Fri 0615, 0715, 0815 and 1045
        Sat and Sun – 0845

Marinecall

Marinecall 2-day forecasts ☎ 09068 500458 for
the southwest at 60p per minute from land
lines.

MRCC Falmouth

VHF Channels 86 for Scilly and local sea areas
at 0110, 0410, 0710, 1010, 1610, 1910 and
2210 UTC

Navtex

Weather bulletins transmitted from Niton (E) at 0840 and 2040 with an extended outlook at 0040 (518 kHz). Inshore forecasts, plus a national 3 day outlook for inshore waters are transmitted from Niton (I) at 0520 and 1720 (490 kHz). All times UT.

Radio France (in French). All times UT.

Weather messages 162 kHz Sat and Sun at 0654 and 2003. 711kHz and 1404kHz at 0640. Useful information on www.guidemanche.com

Port Radio

All times LT.

Falmouth

VHF Ch 12, 0900 – 1700 extended in season.
☎ 01326 312285

Penzance

VHF Ch 12, 0900 – 1700 and 2hr before HW –1hr after HW. ☎ 01736 366113

Newlyn

VHF Ch 16, 12, 0800 – 1700 and overnight emergency service. ☎ 01736 362523

St Mary's

VHF Ch 16, 14, 0800 – 1700 extended in season. ☎ 01720 422768

In addition to the weekday hours, the harbour offices provide extended cover on VHF at weekends and in season.

Weather information via Internet and fax

The UK Met Office offers services on their web site www.metoffice.gov.uk . Inshore waters forecasts are also available at www.marinecall.co.uk for 24H with outlook for following 24H. This information is also available by telephone (£0.60 per minute from UK land line) on ☎ 09068 500458 and by *Fax* in two formats – Standard on ☎ 09060 100458 (£1.00 per minute) or Advance with 5 day outlook on ☎ 09065 300258 (£1.50 per minute).

GRIB files enable free download of computer generated arrow diagram forecasts for any area in the world. Can be viewed on line at www.grib.us. Alternatively, the highly compressed data can be obtained by email using marine HF receiver or satellite telephone.

Other sources of free weather information available on the internet include:
www.bbc.co.uk/weather/coast/shipping
www.passageweather.com
www.oceanweather.com
www.ecmwf.com
www.magicseaweed.com
www.windguru.cz www.xcweather.co.uk
www.weatheronline.co.uk

Navigational aids and safety

Major lights and fog signals at or near Scilly

Bishop Rock

Fl(2)15s44m20M Racon Heli-platform. Grey round granite tower. Partially obscured 204°-211°, obscured 211°-233°, 236°-259°

St Mary's

2 rows F.R lights on TV mast 119m near Telegraph Tower. F.R lights on radio mast on control tower at airport and mast S of airfield

Peninnis Head

Fl.20s36m17M White round metal tower on black metal framework tower, black cupola 231°-vis-117°, part obscured 048°-083° within 5M

Round Island

N side Fl.10s55m18M. Horn(4)60s Racon White round tower 021°-vis-288° Continuous

Lizard E tower

Fl.3s70m26M Horn 30s White 8-sided tower at E end of building 120°-vis-250° A continuous light of low power may sometimes be seen within 12M

Tater-du

Fl(3)15s34m20M Horn(2)30s White round tower 241°-vis-074° F.R.31m13M 060°-vis-074° over Runnel Stone and in places 074°-077° within 4M

Wolf Rock

Fl.15s34m16M Horn 30s Racon Grey round granite tower, black lantern Heli-platform Continuous

Longships

Fl(2)WR.10s35m15/11M Horn 30s Racon Grey round granite tower on highest rock 189°-R-208°-R(unintens)-307°-R-327°-W-189° Helicopter platform Continuous.
F.R on radio mast 4·9M NE

Pendeen

Fl(4)15s59m16M Horn 20s White round tower and dwellings 042°-vis-240°

Seven Stones

LtF Fl(3)30s12m15M Horn(3)60s Racon. Red hull, light-tower amidships. Continuous

Beacons in Scilly

St Martin's Daymark tower

(56m) red and white bands on E end of island

St Mary's Pool Ldg beacons

097° Front: White triangle on a pyramid base. Rear: Red St Andrew's Cross on a pole. The front triangle has Iso.RW(vert))2s and the rear Oc.WR(vert)10s at night

St Agnes old Lighthouse
White tower in centre of island

Crow Rock beacon, Crow Sound
Isolated danger beacon (11m). Black, red, black, **፧** topmark, stands on a rock (dries 4·6m) Fl(2)10s.

Woolpack Point, St Mary's Sound
S card, yellow over black with ▼ topmark

Hulman beacon
S entrance to New Grimsby Sound.
Green ▲ radar reflector on pole Fl.G.6s

Little Rag Ledge beacon
300m to NNW of above, red ■ radar reflector on pole Fl(2)R5s

Bartholomew Ledges, St Mary's Sound
Red beacon. Q.R.

Buoyage

The buoyage on this section of coast is the IALA maritime buoyage system 'A' as shown in the table below. Both the lateral and cardinal systems are in use. All buoys listed below have radar reflectors.

Search and Rescue Services in the SW

All services are co-ordinated by the Maritime Rescue Co-ordination Centre (MRCC) at Falmouth. They maintain continuous watch on DSC MF(2187.5kHz), DSC Channel 70 as well as Channel 16. Their working channels are 06, 10, 23, 67 and 73. The area of Scilly is covered by channels 16 and 23 from a remote station at St Mary's.

Customs clearance

There is no Customs Office in Scilly. Non-EU yachts or yachts with non-EU crew should fly flag Q and telephone ✆0800 7231110 to clear in.

Lifeboats

Lifeboats are stationed as follows: Cadgwith (Lizard); Penlee; St Ives; Sennen Cove; St Mary's (Isles of Scilly).

Hazards and restrictions

Overfalls

There are some overfalls around the islands and there are many smaller overfalls in the sounds and channels which appear when the local current is opposed to a strong wind.

Fishing hazards

A lot of fishing takes place along this part of the coast and a careful watch is necessary in order to avoid fishing boats and their gear which may stretch in any direction. The following types of fishing may be met with:

Trawling

Boats of up to 30m are used for trawling and dredging for fish and scallops. They are hampered by their gear and must be given a good berth. Sometimes they work in pairs with gear between.

Drifting

Boats of up to 13m are used, usually at night, in drifting for herring, mackerel and pilchard. They operate with trains of nets extending up to 2M supported on the surface by small floats, the end being marked by a lighted can buoy. The vessels usually have a small mizzen sail and should be passed to leeward.

Long lining

Lines which can extend up to 7M are laid along the sea bed and are marked by lighted can buoys at intervals. The small boats which lay the lines usually stay in position with their gear.

Trolling

In the spring, summer and autumn, fleets of small boats will be seen trolling for mackerel with hand lines which extend only some 10m behind the boat. A few of the boats will be stationary, 'jigging' for mackerel. The area where this fishing is taking place should be avoided if possible.

Buoys

Name	Location	Type	Topmark	Colour	Remarks	Lights
Hats	Crow Sound	Card S	▼	Y over B	Off S edge shoal (cover 0·4m)	VQ(6)+LFl.10s
Old Wreck	N of Annet	Card N	▲	B over Y	Rock (covers 1m) 150m to S	VQ
Gunner	Broad Sound	Card S	▼	Y over B	Awash rock 300m to N	
Round Rock	Broad Sound	Card N	▲	B over Y	Rock (dries 2·4m) 300m to S	
N Bartholomew	St Mary's Sound	Can light	■	R	Rock (covers 3.4m) 50m SW	Fl.R.5s
Spanish Ledge	St Mary's Sound	Card E	◆	BYB	Rocks awash & covered 200m to W	Q(3)10s Bell
Steeple Rock	NW Passage	Card W	✕	YBY	Rock (covers 0.1m) 300m NE	Q(9)15s
Spencers Ledge	SW Samson	Card S	▼	Y over B	Shoal water to N	Q(6)+LFl.15s
Bacon Ledge	St Mary's Pool	Can light	■	R	Shoal (covers 0.3m) NE	Fl(4)R.5s

Seining

A fishing vessel encircles a shoal of fish with a purse-shaped net supported by floats. When the circle has been completed the ends of the net are joined and drawn in. Nets may be 400m long and at a depth of 75m or more.

Pelagic fishing

Midwinter single and pair trawling and seining September to March. Up to 50 vessels may be encountered in a small area.

Crab pots and tangle netting

Fleets (lines) of pots are set on the sea bottom to catch shellfish. The pots can be set singly, but are usually in lines ½M long, marked by can or other types of buoy, which must be avoided as the gear is very heavy and will damage propellers, etc. In strong tides the buoys are often underwater and difficult to see. This is the major fishing hazard to yachts in the vicinity of the islands.

Diving

Professional and amateur divers operate regularly in the islands, usually near rocks or wrecks. The parent boat should be in the immediate vicinity of the divers. This flies the International Code flag 'A' (white and blue vertical halves, swallow tail). The area should be given a wide berth and a sharp lookout kept for any divers surfacing up to 1M away.

Experimental area

An experimental area 1M square exists 1M to NW of Shipman Head, Bryher. Anchoring and fishing are prohibited. See plan page 42–43.

Historic wrecks

There are many wreck sites around the islands. Three are designated historic wreck sites; one is at Tearing Ledge (see plan page 18), one at Bartholomew Ledges (see plan page 23) and one to the S of Green Island off Samson (see plan page 43). Anchoring, fishing and diving are forbidden near these areas; seek local advice.

Underwater cables

There are many underwater power and telephone cables which have been laid between individual islands and also to the mainland. Where these cables come ashore, there are beacons with yellow diamond topmarks (see plans for details). The sea is usually so clear that cables may be visible on the sea bed. However, it is strongly recommended that anchors are buoyed so that a trip line is available to recover the anchor if necessary.

Exercise area

There is a submarine exercise area to the S of and between Lands End and Scilly and a Firing Practice Area to the S and E of Lizard Point.

Traffic Separation Schemes

See page 13.

Restricted landings

To protect wildlife, in particular breeding birds and seals, landing is not allowed on specific islands on a permanent basis and on others on a seasonal basis without a written permit from the Isles of Scilly Wildlife Trust, St Mary's. The islands which are permanently closed are: Western Rocks (including Annet), Norrard Rocks, Men-a-vaur, Round Island, Hanjague, Great and Little Innisvouls and Menewethan. Those which are seasonally closed from 15 April to 20 August are Samson west North Hill, Samson south end, Samson White Island, Samson Green Island, Samson Stony Island, Bryher Shipman Head, Peashopper Island, Foreman Island, Crow Island, Eastern Isles Ragged Island, Great Ganilly (south end) and Gugh (NE coast and S carns).

Isles of Scilly Wildlife Trust

All of the uninhabited islands and untenanted parts of the islands are now managed by the Isles of Scilly Wildlife Trust, a charity with trustees all based on the islands. This accounts for about 60% of the islands' land area. The Trust's job is to manage this land, to preserve and protect the wildlife of the islands and in the waters around Scilly and to conserve or restore habitats, landscape and archaeological sites for the benefit and enjoyment of the public.

☏ 01720 422153

www.ios-wildlifetrust.org.uk

Marine animal strandings

For live strandings call British Divers Marine Life Rescue ☏ 01825 765546 and for dead strandings call Marine Strandings Hotline. ☏ 08452 012626

Area of Outstanding Natural Beauty

The islands were designated an area of outstanding natural beauty in 1976.

www.ios-aonb.info

Charts

Admiralty 34, 883, 1148, 2565, SC5603
French 6745, 7108
Imray 2400.1, 2400.2, 2400.3, C7, C10, C18

Magnetic variation

3°40′W (2010) decreasing by 09′ each year.

Bearings

All bearings in this book are 'true'.

2. APPROACHES TO SCILLY

Main Anchorages

See plan page 18–19

Skippers arriving for the first time in the Isles of Scilly are likely to head for one of the following main anchorages.

Southern Anchorages

St Mary's Pool
See page 29. Approach ⊕10, 11, 12, 13

Porth Cressa
See page 31. Approach ⊕ 10 and 11

The Cove
See page 71. Approach ⊕10 and 11

Northern Anchorages

New Grimsby Sound
See page 49. Outer Approach ⊕20.

Traffic Separation Schemes

A Traffic Separation Scheme (TSS) lies N/S between Land's End and the Seven Stones and a red light float with a light tower (Fl(3)30s12m15M Racon) guards the western edge of the TSS about two miles NE of the Seven Stones. This infamous reef is the only such hazard in the outer approaches to Scilly and should be given a wide berth. Do not pass between the light float and the rocks.

Traffic Separation Schemes also exist to the S and W of the Isles of Scilly. These schemes require traversing yachts to present the whole of their length at 90° to traffic using the separation scheme. Whatever the wind and tide are doing, yachts must maintain a right-angled appearance so there is no doubt of their intention to cross the TSS by the shortest distance, even if, in so doing, the vessel makes good a diagonal course. If under sail in light winds, an engine, if available, should be used to speed the crossing.

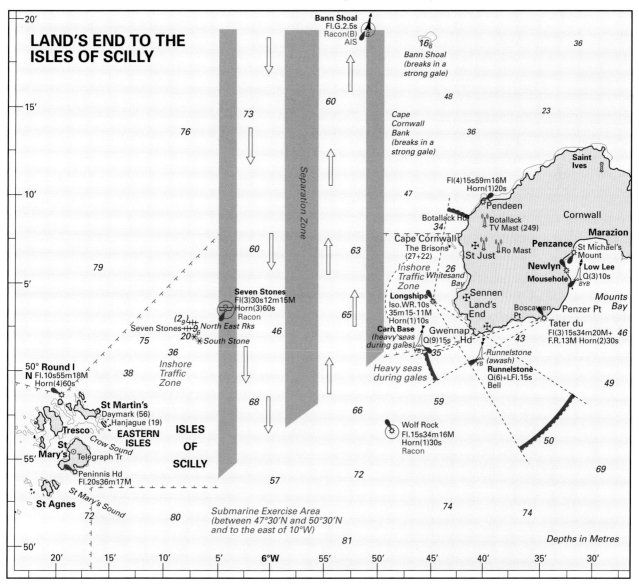

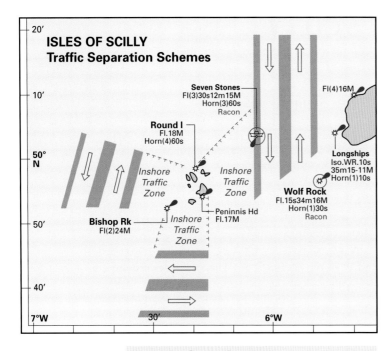

ISLES OF SCILLY
Traffic Separation Schemes

Seven Stones
Fl(3)30s12m15M
Horn(3)60s
Racon

Fl(4)16M

Round I
Fl.18M
Horn(4)60s

Inshore
Traffic
Zone

Inshore
Traffic
Zone

Longships
Iso.WR.10s
35m15-11M
Horn(1)10s

Wolf Rock
Fl.15s34m16M
Horn(1)30s
Racon

Peninnis Hd
Fl.17M

Bishop Rk
Fl(2)24M

Inshore
Traffic
Zone

Passage from the East

The passage from the E, the UK mainland, requires careful calculation of the time of departure so as to arrive in Scilly with enough time to go to anchor in daylight.

With a fair wind at the start of the westbound stream, an early morning departure from, say, the Helford River, makes it possible for most cruising yachts to arrive at Scilly in daylight.

One should leave an anchorage off Penzance or Newlyn at first light if possible and a departure from Land's End at around half ebb (HW Dover −3 hours) towards a point S of Scilly should maximise the use of the tide.

A night passage with arrival before daylight is also practical from points of departure on mainland Britain, and this arrival time is very worthwhile when coming across the English Channel from the S or SE (see page 15).

When on passage from mainland anchorages off Newlyn and Penzance, the Runnel Stone, yellow and black south cardinal bell and whistle buoy (Q(6)+LFl.15s) with ▼ topmark, must be left to starboard and a wide berth should be given to the Longships rocks which lie due W of Land's End about one mile offshore. The Longships lighthouse (Fl(2)WR.10s35m15/11M Horn(1)10s) stands on the tallest rock, and consists of a grey granite tower with a helicopter landing pad.

When on passage westward from the Lizard, Wolf Rock lies almost directly on the course to Scilly. It has a lighthouse (Fl.15s34m16M Horn(1)30s) consisting of a grey round granite tower with black lantern and a helicopter landing pad. It is built on a rock (dries 3–4m) which is steep-to. This lighthouse is very useful for navigating the passage, but one should avoid the heavy overfalls which occur in bad weather to the W of the rock with wind against tide.

If you have the advantage of having fixed your position before dawn then an arrival at Scilly with the sun behind you has much to recommend it, provided visibility is good. Subsequent observation of the daymarks on St Martin and St Agnes (see page 17) together with Bishop Rock lighthouse (Fl(2)15s44m20M Racon (T)) will much assist entry. Yachtsmen approaching Scilly with this light on a bearing of 261°(line AZ) or to ⊕10, before and after dawn are in a good position to make a satisfactory landfall in southern Scilly.

Longships lighthouse, Runnel Stone buoy and Land's End looking NW on passage to Scilly

Bishop Rock lighthouse looking E with St Agnes behind

Wolf Rock lighthouse looking NE

Sea ferry and helicopter services operate between Penzance and the islands; there are also fixed-wing aircraft from Land's End and, in the holiday season, from Exeter, Plymouth and Newquay. Usually the aircraft follow the most direct route and offer a rough check on navigation.

Approach from the East

St Mary's Sound offers what is probably the easiest entry to Scilly from the E (and S). St Mary's Sound separates St Mary's from Gugh and St Agnes to the SW. In SW-W-NW winds and swell there may be heavy seas over the shoals at the NW end of the passage and with a strong E-SE wind against tide the passage can be rough and unpleasant. Good visibility is necessary to see the leading marks, but the channel is buoyed and can be used, with care, in poor visibility. There is a minimum depth of 10m and minimum width of 300m on this approach. ⊕11 and ⊕12 may assist in identifying the leading marks.

Yachtsmen approaching from the E can take advantage of the tall, 44m-high Bishop Rock light, the structure of which can be seen from many miles to the E of Scilly. If proceeding to any of the three most useful southern anchorages, which are The Cove, Porth Cressa and St Mary's Pool (on St Mary's), one should keep Bishop Rock light on a bearing of 261° (E from ⊕10). This gives the S coast of St Mary's a wide berth and clears all obstacles on the distant and middle approach. The bearing also transits the southern point of St Agnes and makes an excellent line of approach to The Cove between St Agnes and Gugh.

Crow Sound This approach offers an alternative but a disadvantage is that it is not useable at all states of the tide and does not have the Bishop Rock light to assist in the distant approach. ⊕23 may assist in the approach to Line F (and

then ⊕14 towards the bar). In good visibility, and with enough height of tide, much of this near approach is sheltered from the prevailing W and SW winds.

Approach from the North

Yachtsmen arriving from the N or NW should not have to worry about the Seven Stones rocks which lie well to the E of the approach track. Details of these rocks are shown below and they should be given a wide berth. When arriving from the N, yachtsmen should find it easy to distinguish Round Island, a noticeably hump-backed island with a conspicuous white lighthouse (Fl.10s55m18M) in the middle as long as visibility is reasonable(see photo page 17). Round Island light is also a very good daymark. It should also be possible to recognise the red and white banded daymark on St Martin's (see photo page 17), a little over 2M ESE.

Half a mile WSW of Round Island lie the group of three tall and peculiarly symmetrical rocks called Men-a-Vaur, 19m, 31m and 35m high respectively (see photo page 64). The northern landfall offers a choice of four passages, each leading into anchorages where a yacht may lie always afloat, namely New Grimsby Sound, Old Grimsby Sound, St Helen's Gap and Tean Sound, although St Helen's Gap is not accessible for a period either side of LWS. Even when the wind is in the SW these anchorages should not be approached from the N in heavy weather as overfalls occur over much of the approach, particularly with wind over tide.

The only light in this area is the powerful light on Round Island, which at night is useful for establishing that one is somewhere in the northern approaches to Scilly. However, as there are no other navigation lights or leading lights in the area, visual fixing is impossible, and night-time entry is not recommended.

Using ⊕20 may be helpful to identify the transit into New Grimsby Sound, ⊕21 for the transit N into St Helen's Gap and transit O into Tean Sound with ⊕22 for the transit K as an alternative (see page 60).

Approach from the South

The majority of yachts visiting Scilly in recent years wear the French ensign and the southerly route is therefore the most popular. The distance from Ushant (Ouessant) or Ile Vierge on the coast of Brittany to St Mary's, Scilly, is about 100 miles and only in mid-summer in ideal conditions would most cruising yachtsmen expect to make this crossing in daylight. From S or E of Ushant, the passage is, of course, longer, and at least some of it must normally be made in darkness.

There are no offshore dangers in the southern approach. The conspicuous lighthouse on Bishop Rock should be seen from afar. In the closer approach the old lighthouse on St Agnes will be seen in daylight although it is not lit (see photo page 17).

Fortunately, there is much to be said for arrival at Scilly just after dawn from this direction, given reasonable conditions of sea and visibility. The Isles of Scilly are so low that they can be invisible from ten miles away, but with careful timing yachtsmen can take advantage of the excellent lights available on the southern approach, before making their entry in daylight. At dawn the islands should be well illuminated by the sun and it should be easy to pick out salient features and the main daymarks. Before dawn in fair visibility the powerful light of Bishop Rock will be seen at least twenty miles away on the port bow while Wolf Rock light will appear the same distance away on the starboard bow. After further progress towards St Mary's, both Peninnis Head light and the Seven Stones light should appear (the former dead ahead and the latter about 45° on the starboard bow (by which time Wolf Rock light will be almost abeam to starboard).

Approaching ⊕11 from the southerly quadrant may be helpful for yachts heading for St Mary's pool. See anchorages summarised on page 13).

Approach from the West

The distant approach from the W has no hazards, but it is suggested that those arriving from this direction, especially for the first time or in less than perfect visibility, should opt for a final approach from N or S. The western aspect of Scilly has only one impeccable navigational mark and that is the Bishop Rock lighthouse (Fl(2)15s44m24M Racon(T)). Otherwise the rocky outcrops are daunting, dangerous and largely unrecognisable.

The Broad Sound which leads into Scilly NE of Bishop Rock is anything but broad and although there are four buoys in this approach, the outer two are not lit and they are by no means obvious in poor visibility. If a yacht strays from the narrow paths of entrance, disaster very soon threatens by way of hidden rocks. These dangerous waters, together with the Atlantic swell, are met three or four miles offshore. In addition, tidal streams can run strongly and eddies are unpredictable. Visibility has only to shut down a little to make navigational fixes difficult to obtain. The important anchorages are easier to reach from directions other than W, and, generally speaking, with more safety. If an approach is to be made through Broad Sound then ⊕15 may assist in the identification of the leading marks for transit Line W. (⊕15, 16 and 17 may be helpful.)

Northwest Passage, formerly known as the North Channel, now has two lit buoys, is wide, deep and presents little difficulty, but requires good visibility because the leading marks and points used for navigational fixes are distant (establish transit line V using ⊕19 and line W using ⊕16). Tidal streams are strong and run across the line of approach. There are no suitable anchorages except Porth Conger (St Agnes) or St Mary's Pool. Minimum depth 10.4m, minimum width 1300m.

Warning Heavy breaking seas occur in gale conditions over the two 12–3m shoals located ¾M and 1M to NNW of Annet and in line with the leading marks. Overfalls occur over and near the rocky shallows to SW of this channel. There is a strong tide rip to NW of Steeple Rock during NW-going spring tides. There is a Traffic Separation Zone to NW of the approach

Otherwise, for yachtsmen arriving from a westerly quadrant the wisest choice is either to give the Northern ('Norrard') Rocks good clearance and take the New Grimsby Sound approach (see page 45) or to enter from the S (see above) This decision is most likely to be based on an assessment of the probable wind direction when the yacht is eventually at anchor; the northern anchorages being more comfortable in winds from W through S, and the southern anchorages (with the important exception of St Mary's Pool) in winds from W through N. As can be seen from the wind roses on page 5 winds from an easterly quadrant are not common in the summer months. Shelter may be obtained from such winds in all the main anchorages detailed, although swell may become a problem in The Cove and Porth Cressa if strong easterlies persist, and these places should be evacuated if the wind veers to the SE.

When arriving at the southern anchorages from the W, it is important to give Bishop Rock a wide berth. For those yachtsmen arriving from this direction for the first time, it is worth remembering that there are no points of recognition on the Retarrier Ledges, the extensive Western Rocks, Gorregan, Melledgan or Annet. The best approach tactic is to keep well clear of the area. Yachtsmen should aim to leave Bishop Rock light about 3 miles clear to the N, at which point the old lighthouse, a white daymark, on St Agnes will bear NE. (This position is only a mile E of Pol Bank with a charted depth of 23m, on which seas can break in rough or very rough weather.) Alter course to steer E and approach the land when the old lighthouse bears N. Then bear away to the NE when St Agnes island is about a mile off and proceed to one of the anchorages. For southern anchorages see pages 29, 31 and 76).

3. LEADING LINES, PROMINENT MARKS AND MAIN WAYPOINTS

The leading lines and their descriptions for entry and passage within the Islands are shown on pages 18 and 19.

The most useful fixed navigational marks in the islands are two tall, well maintained and brightly painted daymarks; one is the old white lighthouse building on St Agnes (49m) and the other is the red and white horizontally banded daymark (56m) at the NE end of St Martin's. Because of their colouring and position one or both of these unlit marks can, in reasonable visibility, be seen on most of the approaches to and within Scilly and they show up more readily in binoculars than less conspicuous objects. They are most helpful in approaches from S and E when both offer position checks by compass.

These two marks have been carefully preserved since the 1680s and testify to the trust which mariners have placed in them for over 300 years.

St Agnes old lighthouse

St Martin's Daymark and ruins of Napoleonic signal station

One other useful and prominent mark is Round Island lighthouse (55m) and this white tower on a distinctive rock is also an excellent daymark, particularly helpful when making an approach from the N.

By contrast, the charted high marks on St Mary's (notably the TV tower and the grey stone telegraph tower) can be curiously indistinguishable at a distance, particularly against a background of cloud, although the TV tower can be a useful component of transits when navigating among the islands. There is also a daymark (43m) on top of Watch Hill, Bryher (see photo below), but unfortunately it is less brightly painted than those on St Agnes and St Martin's. This mark needs to be observed well before closing the coast as it disappears under the high ground of Shipman Head. Nonetheless, the mark does offer those arriving from N or NW a useful check on their position during the approach.

Round Island and its lighthouse *Mike Lewin-Harris*

Hangman I   Daymark (Bryher)

The daymark on Watch Hill (Bryher), looking SSW from above Cromwell's Castle (Tresco)

TV tower, St Mary's

Telegraph Tower, St Mary's

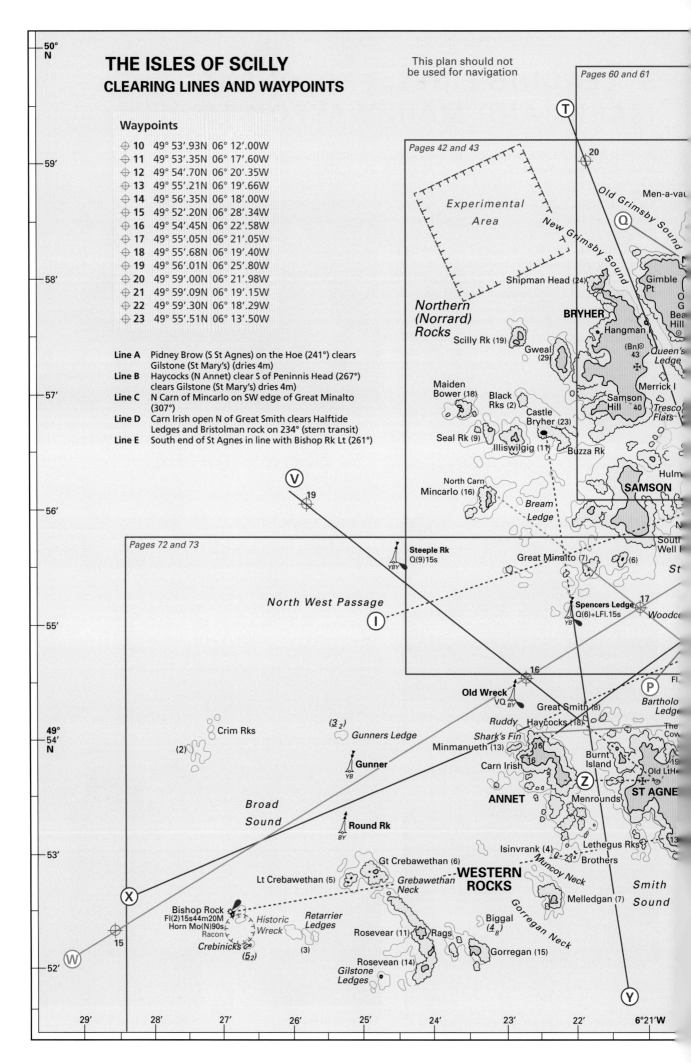

THE ISLES OF SCILLY
CLEARING LINES AND WAYPOINTS

This plan should not be used for navigation

Pages 60 and 61

Waypoints

⊕ 10 49° 53'.93N 06° 12'.00W
⊕ 11 49° 53'.35N 06° 17'.60W
⊕ 12 49° 54'.70N 06° 20'.35W
⊕ 13 49° 55'.21N 06° 19'.66W
⊕ 14 49° 56'.35N 06° 18'.00W
⊕ 15 49° 52'.20N 06° 28'.34W
⊕ 16 49° 54'.45N 06° 22'.58W
⊕ 17 49° 55'.05N 06° 21'.05W
⊕ 18 49° 55'.68N 06° 19'.40W
⊕ 19 49° 56'.01N 06° 25'.80W
⊕ 20 49° 59'.00N 06° 21'.98W
⊕ 21 49° 59'.09N 06° 19'.15W
⊕ 22 49° 59'.30N 06° 18'.29W
⊕ 23 49° 55'.51N 06° 13'.50W

Line A   Pidney Brow (S St Agnes) on the Hoe (241°) clears Gilstone (St Mary's) (dries 4m)
Line B   Haycocks (N Annet) clear S of Peninnis Head (267°) clears Gilstone (St Mary's) dries 4m)
Line C   N Carn of Mincarlo on SW edge of Great Minalto (307°)
Line D   Carn Irish open N of Great Smith clears Halftide Ledges and Bristolman rock on 234° (stern transit)
Line E   South end of St Agnes in line with Bishop Rk Lt (261°)

Pages 42 and 43

Experimental Area

New Grimsby Sound

Old Grimsby Sound

Men-a-vau

Shipman Head (24)

Northern (Norrard) Rocks

Scilly Rk (19)

Gweal (29)

Maiden Bower (18)

Black Rks (2)

Castle Bryher (23)

Seal Rk (9)

Illiswilgig (11)

Buzza Rk

North Carn Mincarlo (16)

Bream Ledge

Great Minalto (7)

(6)

BRYHER

Gimble Pt

Hangman

(Bn) 43

Queen's Ledge

Merrick I

Samson Hill 40

Tresco Flats

SAMSON

Hulm

South Well

Pages 72 and 73

Steeple Rk
Q(9)15s
YBY

North West Passage

Spencers Ledge
Q(6)+LFl.15s
YB

Woodco

17

V
19

I

16

Old Wreck
VQ BY

Great Smith (8)

Ruddy   Haycocks (18)

Shark's Fin

Minmanueth (13)

Carn Irish

ANNET

Menrounds

Burnt Island

Old LtHo

ST AGNE

Bartholo Ledge

P

The Cow

Z

Crim Rks

(2)

(3₂)   Gunners Ledge

Gunner
YB

Broad Sound

Round Rk
BY

Gt Crebawethan (6)

Lt Crebawethan (5)   Grebawethan Neck

Bishop Rock
Fl(2)15s44m20M
Horn Mo(N)90s
Racon

Retarrier Ledges

Rosevear (11)   Rags

Historic Wreck

Crebinicks
(5₂)

(3)

Rosevean (14)
Gilstone Ledges

WESTERN ROCKS

Isinvrank (4)

Brothers

Muncoy Neck

Biggal (4₈)

Gorregan (15)

Melledgan (7)

Lethegus Rks

Smith Sound

Gorregan Neck

X
W
15

Y

18 ISLES OF SCILLY

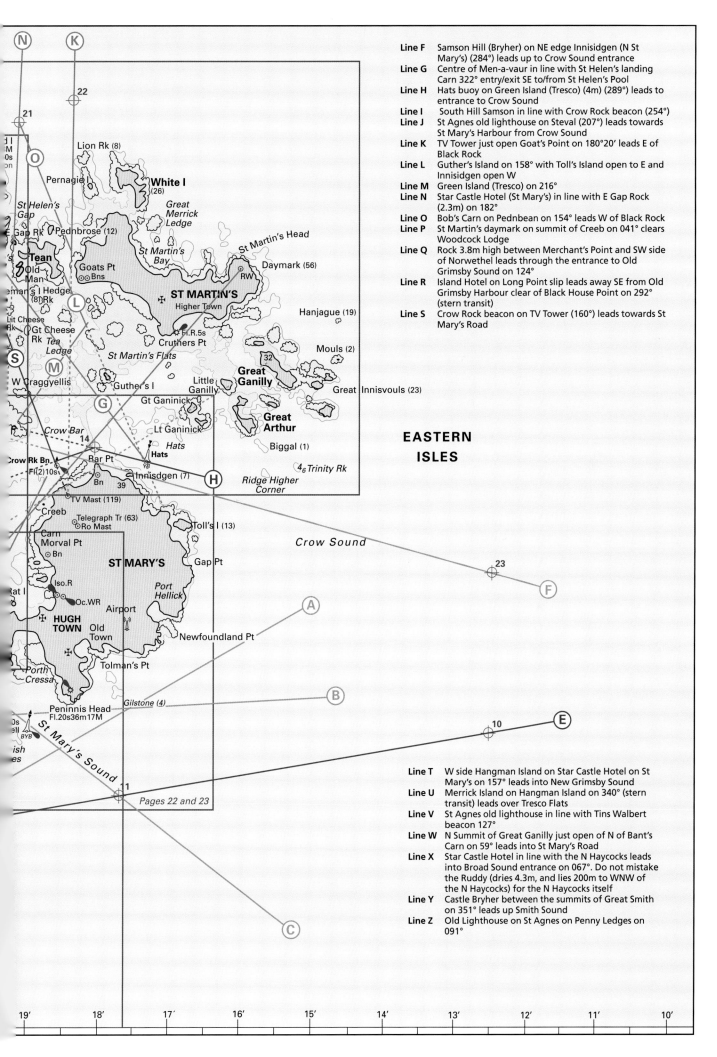

Line F Samson Hill (Bryher) on NE edge Innisidgen (N St Mary's) (284°) leads up to Crow Sound entrance

Line G Centre of Men-a-vaur in line with St Helen's landing Carn 322° entry/exit SE to/from St Helen's Pool

Line H Hats buoy on Green Island (Tresco) (4m) (289°) leads to entrance to Crow Sound

Line I South Hill Samson in line with Crow Rock beacon (254°)

Line J St Agnes old lighthouse on Steval (207°) leads towards St Mary's Harbour from Crow Sound

Line K TV Tower just open Goat's Point on 180°20' leads E of Black Rock

Line L Guther's Island on 158° with Toll's Island open to E and Innisidgen open W

Line M Green Island (Tresco) on 216°

Line N Star Castle Hotel (St Mary's) in line with E Gap Rock (2.3m) on 182°

Line O Bob's Carn on Pednbean on 154° leads W of Black Rock

Line P St Martin's daymark on summit of Creeb on 041° clears Woodcock Lodge

Line Q Rock 3.8m high between Merchant's Point and SW side of Norwethel leads through the entrance to Old Grimsby Sound on 124°

Line R Island Hotel on Long Point slip leads away SE from Old Grimsby Harbour clear of Black House Point on 292° (stern transit)

Line S Crow Rock beacon on TV Tower (160°) leads towards St Mary's Road

EASTERN
ISLES

Line T W side Hangman Island on Star Castle Hotel on St Mary's on 157° leads into New Grimsby Sound

Line U Merrick Island on Hangman Island on 340° (stern transit) leads over Tresco Flats

Line V St Agnes old lighthouse in line with Tins Walbert beacon 127°

Line W N Summit of Great Ganilly just open of N of Bant's Carn on 59° leads into St Mary's Road

Line X Star Castle Hotel in line with the N Haycocks leads into Broad Sound entrance on 067°. Do not mistake the Ruddy (dries 4.3m, and lies 200m to WNW of the N Haycocks) for the N Haycocks itself

Line Y Castle Bryher between the summits of Great Smith on 351° leads up Smith Sound

Line Z Old Lighthouse on St Agnes on Penny Ledges on 091°

View SSE over St Mary's Pool with Hugh Town,
Scillonian III **alongside, visitors' moorings (left) and**
Porth Cressa (top right) *Patrick Roach*

St Mary's

OVERVIEW

St Mary's is the largest of the Isles of Scilly and covers an area of 629 hectares (1 hectare = 10,000m^2); it measures about two and a half miles across at its widest point and has a coastline of over 9 miles. The island has a population of about 1,500 permanent residents, about 80% of the total population of Scilly, although this number is swelled by about 100,000 visitors to Scilly each year, some staying on the island and others passing on to other islands. There are two main anchorages on the Island: St Mary's Pool, N of Hugh Town, is the principal harbour for the islands and offers shelter from the S and E but is exposed to the W through to N. The second is Porth Cressa which is open to the S and uncomfortable in SE but relatively sheltered from NW through to NE.

PASSAGES

The easiest and best marked passage into the main anchorages of St Mary's from the mainland, and also from the south, is through St Mary's Sound between Gugh and St Mary's. An alternative approach from the east is through Crow Sound when weather and tides permit and alternative passages for experienced yachtsmen approaching from the south are Smith Sound, Broad Sound and the North West Passage (formerly known as the 'North Channel').

St Mary's Sound

Lighthouses, buoys and beacons

Bishop Rock lighthouse
Fl(2)15s44m20M. Racon (T)

Peninnis Head lighthouse
Fl.20s36m17M

Spanish Ledge
East cardinal Bell buoy. Black, yellow, black with ♦ topmark. Q(3)10s

Woolpack
South cardinal beacon. Yellow and black with ♦ topmark

Bartholomew Ledges
Red beacon on shoal (0.6m). Q.R.

N Bartholomew
Red can buoy. Fl.R.5s

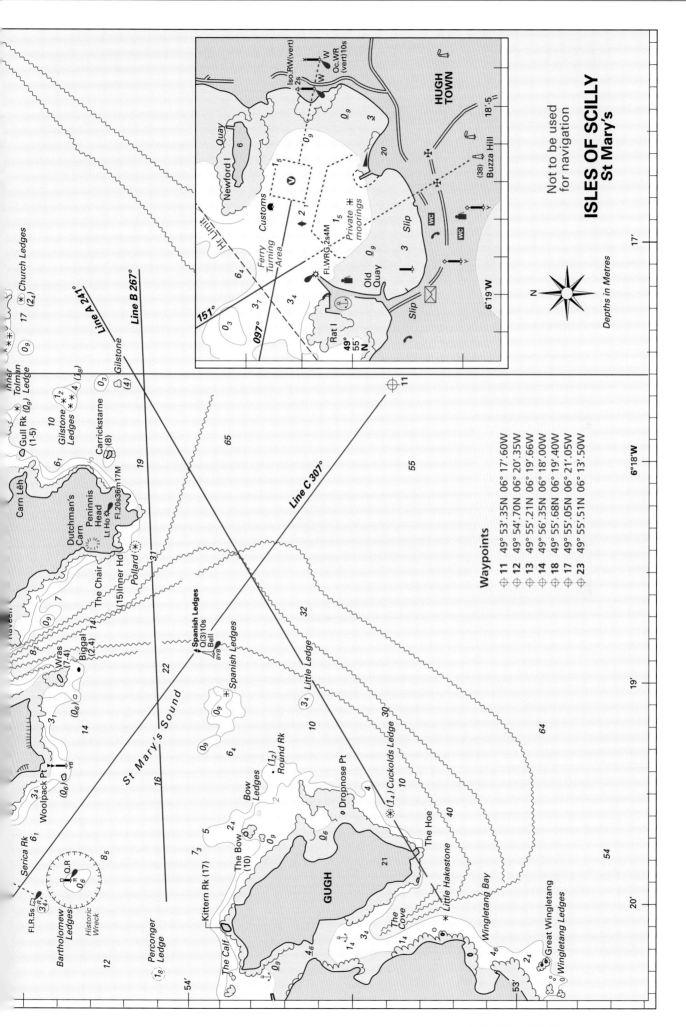

ISLES OF SCILLY
St Mary's

Not to be used
for navigation

Depths in Metres

6°19'W

HUGH TOWN

18·5

Buzza Hill
(38)

WC

WC

Private ⌖
moorings

Slip

3

Old
Quay

0·9

3

Slip

Rat I

49°
55'
N

097°
151°
Hr Limit

Ferry
Turning
Area

Customs

Fl.WR.G.2s4M
6·4
3·1
3·4

0·3

Newford I

Quay

6

0·9

Iso.RW(vert)
2s
W W

Oc.WR
(vert)10s

1·5

2·1

0·9

3

20

1·5

Waypoints

⊕ 11 49° 53'.35N 06° 17'.60W
⊕ 12 49° 54'.70N 06° 20'.35W
⊕ 13 49° 55'.21N 06° 19'.66W
⊕ 14 49° 56'.35N 06° 18'.00W
⊕ 18 49° 55'.68N 06° 19'.40W
⊕ 17 49° 55'.05N 06° 21'.05W
⊕ 23 49° 55'.51N 06° 13'.50W

6°18'W

17'

Inner
Tolman

⊛ Church Ledges
17 (2·4)

Gull Rk ⊛
(1·5) (0·9) Ledge

0·9

Gilstone
Ledges ⊛⊛ 4 (1·8)
10 (1·2)

Gilstone
(4) 0·3

Carn Lêh

Carrickstarne
⊛ (8)

Line A 241°

Line B 267°

6·1

19

65

55

Dutchman's
Carn
Peninnis
Head
Fl.20s36m17M
The Chair Lt Ho ⌖

(15)Inner Hd
Pollard ⊛

31

Line C 307°

7

0·9

8·2

14

Wras
(7·4)

0·6

Biggal
(2·4)

Spanish Ledges
Q(3)10s
Bell
BYB

22

⌖ Spanish Ledges

0·9

6·4

32

Little Ledge

3·4

St Mary's Sound

16

14

3·1

0·6

0·6

Woolpack Pt

YB

Bow
Ledges

0·9
Round Rk
(1·2)

10

(1·4) Cuckolds Ledge
⊛ Dropnose Pt

30

10

Serica Rk

6·1

3·4

Q.R
R
0·6

Bartholomew
Ledges

Historic
Wreck

8·5

Kittern Rk (17)

7·3

5

The Bow
(10)

2·4

0·9

0·6

4

The Hoe

Little Hakestone

40

64

54

Fl.R.5s
R
3·4

12

Perconger
Ledge
(1·8)

The Calf

0·9

4·6

GUGH

21

3·4

The Cove

1·4

3·4

1·4

⊛

0

4·6

Great Wingletang
Wingletang Ledges

Wingletang Bay

2·4

20'

53'

N

⚓

⚓

W

W

V

⚓

49°
55'
N

Leading marks

Approach from E

Line E
S end of St Agnes in line Bishop Rock lighthouse on 261°. The easiest approach to St Mary's Sound - from ⊕10 and ⊕11

Line B
Haycocks (N Annet) clear S of Peninnis Head (267°) clears Gilstone (St Mary's). Dries 4m

Approach from NE

Line A
Pidney Brow (S St Agnes) on The Hoe (241°) clears Gilstone (St Mary's). Dries 4m – from ⊕23

Through St Mary's Sound

Line C
N Carn of Mincarlo on SW edge of Great Minalto (307°) through ⊕11 and ⊕12

St Mary's Road

Line P
St Martin's Daymark on summit of Creeb 041° clears Woodcock Ledge, ⊕12, 13

North Bartholomew buoy and the N Carn of Mincarlo in line with W extremity of Great Minalto

Directions

Yachtsmen approaching from the E can take advantage of the tall, 44m high, Bishop Rock lighthouse, the structure of which can be seen for many miles to the E of Scilly. If proceeding to any of the three most useful southern anchorages (The Cove, St Agnes, Porth Cressa and St Mary's Pool, St Mary's) one should head towards Bishop Rock lighthouse on a bearing of 261° (line E). This gives the S coast of St Mary's a wide berth and clears all obstacles on the distant and middle approach. The bearing also transits the southern point of St Agnes and makes an excellent line of approach to The Cove which lies between St Agnes and Gugh.

Approach St Mary's from the E ⊕10, heading for the Bishop Rock light (over S tip of St Agnes) on a course of 261°. When Peninnis Head lighthouse bears approximately 335°, distant about one mile,⊕11 alter course to 307° (⊕12) on the charted transit (Line C) of the N Carn of Mincarlo in line with the W extremity of Great Minalto (See diagram page 25 and photo below).

The names of these two rocks are misleading because the N Carn of Mincarlo is much bigger than the tiny rock of Great Minalto and this can cause confusion. If in doubt about the transit identify the Spanish Ledge Buoy which lies close to port of the transit line. Spanish Ledge is an E Cardinal bell buoy, black and yellow with a black ♦ topmark (Q(3)10s) marking a group of covered rocks, one of which is awash at LAT.

When the buoy lies close abeam to port alter course due N to enter Port Cressa or continue on the transit line (307°) past Woolpack Point to starboard where there is a S cardinal beacon, yellow over black ♦ (7m) standing close to a rock which dries 0.6m and then leave the lit beacon and red can buoy on Bartholomew Ledges close abeam to port. The beacon is QR and the buoy Fl.R.5s marking some rocks that cover 0.6m. Continue on this course until the

Buzza Hill Tower   Hospital chimney

Porth Cressa from seaward with Wras and Biggal in the foreground

Tidal streams

In St Mary's Sound:

Local HW	Plymouth HW	Dover HW	Direction	Rate (knots)	
				Spring	Neaps
-0505	-0600	+0045	NW	0.4	0.2
-0205	-0300	+0345	ESE	1.2	0.5
+0055	0000	-0540	ESE	1.7	0.8
+0355	+0300	-0240	W	1.3	0.6
+0555	+0600	+0020	WNW	0.7	0.3

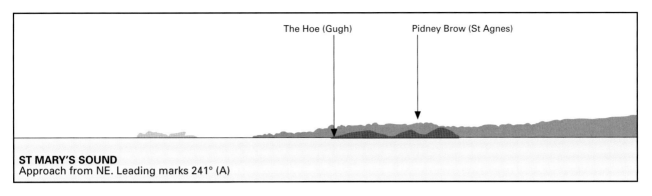

ST MARY'S SOUND
Approach from NE. Leading marks 241° (A)

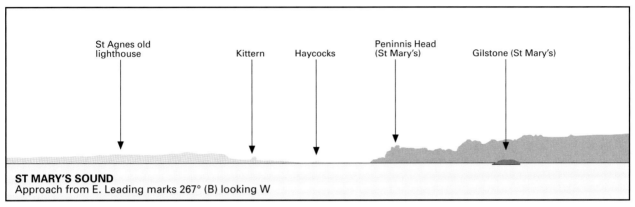

ST MARY'S SOUND
Approach from E. Leading marks 267° (B) looking W

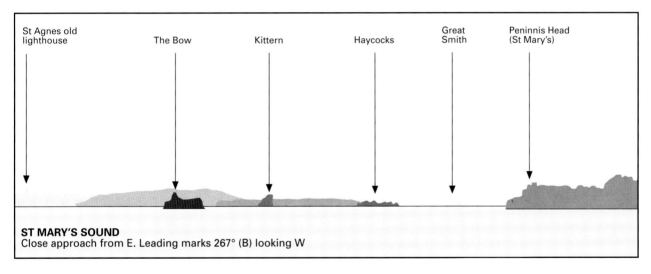

ST MARY'S SOUND
Close approach from E. Leading marks 267° (B) looking W

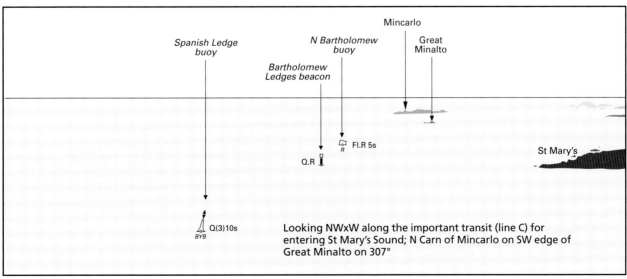

Looking NWxW along the important transit (line C) for entering St Mary's Sound; N Carn of Mincarlo on SW edge of Great Minalto on 307°

Woolpack beacon in the approach to St Mary's Pool with Steval (left)

Bartholomew   Old lighthouse
Ledges beacon   St Agnes

N Bartolemew

**View SW over approach to St Mary's with Bartholomew Ledges beacon,
N Bartholomew and St Agnes in the background**

day mark at the E end of St Martin's bears 041° and is in transit with Creeb, the westernmost rock on the NW coast of St Mary's ⊕12. Alter course to starboard onto this transit (Line P, 041°) for about ¾ mile to clear Woodcock Ledge to the SE. ⊕13 and ⊕14 may assist in identifying the transit. This leads to three possible approaches to St Mary's Pool (See Main anchorages and moorings below).

Crow Sound

This sound is located on the NE side of St Mary's and separates it from St Martin's and the Eastern Isles. The sound has a very wide entrance and is funnel-shaped, leading to a narrow passage over Crow Bar into St Mary's Road. It is easy to locate and enter and, if the wind is in the S or W, there is a good anchorage off Watermill Cove where vessels may wait for sufficient water to cross Crow Bar. The Watermill Cove anchorage is untenable with winds from E-SE but sheltered from other directions. ⊕23 may assist in identifying the leading marks which are distant and require good visibility but the sound is buoyed and can be used with care in conditions of reduced visibility when the leading marks cannot be seen. The sound must not be used with gales from E and SE. Minimum depth 0.8m, minimum width 150m.

Buoys and beacons

Hats

S cardinal yellow and black buoy (VQ(6)+LFl.10s) with ⍗ topmark located off S edge of Hats rocky shoal (covers 0.4m) plus the boiler framework of a wreck(dries 0.6m)

Crow Rock

Black, red and black beacon (Fl(2)10s) with ⁑ topmark on an isolated rock (dries 4.6m)

Leading marks

Approach from E and ESE

Line F

Samson Hill (Bryher) on NE edge Innisidgen (N St Mary's) (284°) leads up centre of entrance from ⊕23.(⊕14 and ⊕18 may assist later)

Line G

Centre of Men-a-Vaur in line with St Helen's Landing Carn 322° (see photo page 64)

Line H

Hats buoy on Green Island (Tresco)(4m) 289° leads up centre of entrance, ⊕14 and then ⊕18 (may assist)

Tidal streams

At entrance to Crow Sound:

Local HW	Plymouth HW	Dover HW	Direction	Rate (knots)	
				Spring	Neaps
−0505	−0600	+0045	N	0.9	0.4
−0205	−0300	+0345	NNE	1.7	0.8
+0055	0000	−0540	ESE	0.2	0.1
+0355	+0300	−0240	SSW	2.2	1.0
+0555	+0600	+0020	N	0.7	0.3

Note: Stream reaches 2.9 knot at HW Plymouth +2H in springs.

Crossing of Crow Bar

Line I

South Hill Samson in line with Crow Rock beacon (254°)

Line J

St Agnes old lighthouse on Steval (207°) leads towards St Mary's Harbour from Crow Sound

Warning

There is a tidal race across the entrance to Crow Sound and to the S of St Mary's which extends up to 2M to seaward. This race occurs with the NE-going tidal stream. Local HW −0235, Plymouth −0330, Dover +0330 and with strong NE wind it can be dangerous. Do not attempt, without local knowledge, to cut the corner of the entrance on the N side especially if there is a swell which may break over shallows and shoals.

Directions

Approach Crow Sound using the leading marks (Line F from ⊕23) until Hats buoy ⚑ topmark (VQ(6)+LFl.10s) is located. When it is under 1M away, and if there is sufficient water to clear the bar, approach it on a WNW heading and leave to starboard, turning onto 322° with the centre of Men-a-Vaur in line with St Helen's Landing Carn (Line G). When Crow Rock beacon (Black, red, black. Fl(2)10s) is seen to be on S end of Samson turn towards it and bring South Hill, Samson in line with Crow Rock beacon on 254° (Line I), crossing Crow Bar (0.8m)(⊕14). Crow Rock beacon can be passed

on either side but the N side is recommended. In poor visibility when the leading marks cannot be identified, close the NE side of St Mary's which can always be identified by its telegraph tower and TV tower and follow the coast around to N and NW, keeping 500m from the coast and its inshore islets until Hats buoy is reached. When there is sufficient water to clear the bar leave Hats buoy close to starboard and steer a course for Green Island (SE Tresco) (Line H). This course clears the underwater rocks off Innisidgen by 100m and roughly parallels the coast. Once the transit for line I is lined up proceed as above. From Crow Rock beacon bring St Agnes old lighthouse on to Steval and turn onto line J on 207°.If continuing S to St Mary's Pool take care to clear 'The Cow', an unmarked drying rock W of Taylor's Island.

Crow Rock beacon

Hats Buoy looking WNW with Tresco Abbey and Green Island in the background

North West Passage

See plan page 18

Buoys and beacons

Round Island lighthouse
Fl.10s55m18M Horn(4)60s. Racon(M)

Bishop Rock lighthouse
Fl(2)15s44m20M. Racon(T)

Steeple Rock
West cardinal buoy, yellow, black, yellow with ⅄ topmark. Q(9)15s

Spencers Ledge
South cardinal buoy, yellow and black with ⅄ topmark. Q(6)+LFl.15s

Old Wreck
North cardinal buoy, black and yellow with ⅄ topmark. VQ

Leading marks

Line V
St Agnes old lighthouse in transit with black and white beacon on Tins Walbert 127°, leads through North Channel (from ⊕19 to ⊕16)

Line W
N summit of Great Ganilly just open N of Bant's Carn on 059° leads into St Mary's Road (from ⊕16 to ⊕17)

Directions

Using Round Island, identified by its lighthouse, the isolated Bishop Rock Lighthouse and the old lighthouse on St Agnes obtain a position where the latter bears 130° and Round Island is still clear N of Shipman Head at the N of Bryher. Identify Tins Walbert with its distinctive black and white day mark (see photo below) and approach on 127° (from ⊕19) with St Agnes old lighthouse in line with the beacon(Line V). Leave Steeple Rock W cardinal buoy (yellow, black, yellow with ⅄ topmark Q(9)15s) about 300m to port and, when ½M to N of Annet (⊕16) and, about ¼ M NE of Old Wreck N cardinal buoy (black, yellow with ⅄ topmark VQ) turn onto 059° and approach St Mary's Road with the N summit of Great Ganilly just open N of Bant's Carn (line W, to ⊕17). Spencer's Ledge S cardinal buoy (Q(6)+LFl.15s) lies 200m to port on this approach. If heading for St Mary's Pool a course of about 080°from ⊕17 to a position about 0.2M NW of Newman Island (⊕13) clears Woodcock Ledge and picks up the leading marks for the easiest entry from the W.

Broad Sound and Smith Sound

For directions see page 72 below

St Agnes old lighthouse almost in transit with Tins Walbert beacon (Line V)

Tidal streams

In North West Passage (Spencer's Ledge):

Local HW	Plymouth HW	Dover HW	Direction	Rate (knots) Spring	Neaps
−0505	−0600	+0045	WNW	0.4	0.2
−0205	−0300	+0345	ESE	1.0	0.4
+0055	0000	−0540	SSE	0.2	0.1
+0355	+0300	−0240	WSW	1.2	0.5
+0555	+0600	+0020	WNW	0.5	0.2

Note: Stream reaches 1.5 knots at HW Plymouth + 4H in springs.

MAIN ANCHORAGES AND MOORINGS

St Mary's Pool

See plan page 23

Sheltered NE-E-SE-S-SW. For those arriving for the first time the best arrival is from the west between Bacon Ledge (to the N) and Rat Island (to the S) (Approach 1 on chart at pages 22 and 23). From St Mary's Road ($\oplus$13) The approach is marked by two lit marks in line 097°. The St Mary's lifeboat is almost directly on this approach when she is on station and the two lit marks are in line behind. The lower front mark consists of a white triangle, while the higher mark behind is an orange St Andrew's cross on a tower in the ruined fort known as Harry's Walls above Porthmellon beach on the E side of St Mary's Pool. The upper mark shows Oc.WR(vert)10s and the lower mark shows Iso.RW(vert)2s at night. Follow the bearing 097° until the head of the quay is abeam, then proceed towards the visitors' buoys. There is a three colour sector light on St Mary's pier head to aid night time arrival. The characteristics are as follows: Fl.WRG.2s5m4M 070°-R-100°-W-130°-G-070°.

Alternatively approach from the northwest between Bacon Ledge (to the SW) and The Cow (to the NE) (Approach 2 on chart at pages 22 and 23). A red can buoy is positioned close to the SW of Bacon Ledge (Fl(4)R.5s). This is a good entrance with leading marks in line on 151°. The front leading mark is a small cream shelter with a wide vertical white stripe on a black roof. Look for a building about the size of a bus shelter. It is situated on the edge of the harbour and is not always easy to see (see photo right). The rear mark is a conspicuous squat stone tower (37m) on the skyline of Buzza Hill. There is a stern transit for this entrance with the E edge of Hangman Island on SW edge of Carn Near (Crow Point), Tresco, on 331°. Approach on these lines until the head of the quay is abeam.

From the north approach on 186°, with the white patch at the head of the Old Quay in line

Leading marks for W approach to St Mary's Pool

Leading marks for NW approach to St Mary's Pool

with the grey truncated roof (but see on page 27 warning about 'The Cow', unmarked drying rock). Note that the ferry obscures the front mark when secured alongside the New Quay. On arrival you may pick up a visitors' mooring if one is available but anchoring is not allowed anywhere within the harbour limits which are to the SE of a line joining Newman Island and the W end of Newford Island (see plan on pages 22 and 23). It is wise to approach with your VHF set to Ch.16 as the harbourmaster may wish to give you directions but once within the harbour area contact his staff anyway on Ch.16 (call sign *St Mary's Harbour*) and then go to working Ch.14.

St Mary's Pool from Town Beach
David Lomax

All new arrivals should report to the harbourmaster's office as soon as possible although the staff will be fully occupied when the ferry *Scillonian III* arrives from the mainland. The 41 visitors' mooring buoys and residents' moorings occupy most of the harbour. The holding in this area was never very good and, when the wind veered from W through to NW – following the usual pattern on the passing of a deep depression – the harbour becomes very exposed and it was common for vessels to drag their anchors. These moorings are heavy duty and yachtsmen using them may find their vessels are safer than at anchor. There are 28 moorings for vessels to 40´ (the four inshore trots), 11 for vessels up to 60´ (two outer trots), one for vessels to 80´ and one to 100´. In season visitors may have to 'raft up' and share a mooring buoy, quite possibly with a commercial vessel as there is heavy demand for shelter in bad weather. The charge for one night (2009) was £17 for a vessel to 40´ and £23 for up to 60´. For vessels paying for three nights the fourth is free. The harbour staff visit vessels each morning to collect the fees but request that yachts planning an early departure make payment on the previous day. Cash or a cheque posted through the harbourmaster's door is acceptable! In strong W to NW winds yachts may, if there is a vacant mooring astern, find that they will lie back and bump into it.

The islands are served by boats

St Mary's with the dinghy pontoon, Rat Island and harbourmaster's office

Much of the harbour is occupied by private moorings and almost half this area – the landward side between the quay and the lifeboat slip – dries at low water neaps and the drying part extends almost to the end of the New Quay at Springs. Dinghies may be secured only on the designated pontoon at the corner of the New Quay. If they are left elsewhere they may be moved. The harbour staff are usually happy to give permission for vessels to dry out against the quay just N of the dinghy pontoon if repairs are required. Occasionally demand for this berth necessitates rafting. Long warps are required and crew will need to adjust them as tidal height changes.

Diesel fuel and Petrol are available from pumps close to the centre of the main quay, S of the position where the *Scillonian III* secures alongside, every day except Sundays. Fresh water is also available from the same spot. *Scillonian III* is never alongside between 0800 and 1100 (except occasionally at weekends in August) and the harbour staff will be pleased to advise on your requirements for fuel and water at this time. It is wise to get there early as a queue soon forms in season. Except for a tap at New Grimsby (see page 54) there is no public source of fresh water convenient for yachts anywhere else in Scilly.

Yachtsmen planning to visit other islands would do well to spend some time in St Mary's first, checking out the three transits on the approach to the harbour as the components of each transit can each be seen with little effort. Follow this by a walk up to the Star Castle Hotel to check out the lie of the land from the battlements. It is best to do this at LW and ideally at Springs when great stretches of sand and rocks appear. It is a salutary exercise to envisage how one can walk (perhaps run would be more apt!) between the islands at LWS (except for Gugh/St Agnes which have always been separated by deep water from the rest of the inhabited islands).

A trip on one of the local boats can also be a good way to familiarise yourself with marks and channels before exploring the other islands in your own vessel.

Porth Cressa Bay

Porth Cressa

Sheltered W-NW-N-NE-E. Enter Porth Cressa leaving Biggal (2.4m) about 150m abeam to port. Stand on for a further 100m until The Wras (3.4m) lies abeam to port and then enter the anchorage on a course of about NW. This is a pleasant anchorage offering good shelter in strong NW winds and is convenient for access to Hugh Town although it is a long haul by dinghy from the seaward part of the anchorage to the town at HW. The very limited area of sheltered deep water for fin-keel yachts lies between Raveen and Morning Point and extends about 200m into the harbour which is otherwise shallow or drying. Swell can be unpleasant in Porth Cressa and vessels should leave if wind arrives from the S quadrant. The bottom is sand with rocky patches and depths vary from about 7m W of Raveen to 2m 150m to the NW. Two beacons with yellow diamond topmarks indicate the position of several cables which run across the anchorage from the beach. There are public WCs ashore as well as Sibleys laundry.

Porth Cressa and Hugh Town from The Garrison, St Mary's

Generator Chimney Buzza Hill Tower

**Watermill Cove
and Toll's Island,
St Mary's
looking SE**
Patrick Roach

Watermill Cove

Sheltered S-SW-W-NW. This anchorage is situated on the NE coast of St Mary's and offers fin-keel yachts particularly good shelter in SW winds. Approach on a SW course and tuck in with care among some rocky patches to anchor in about 5m sand. In poor visibility, or if you are unsure of your position, locate Hats buoy and then approach the anchorage on a S course. There is not much room close in but, provided the wind does not shift to NW it is usually possible to find shelter in about 10-12m further offshore. Watermill Cove is also a good spot to wait for sufficient rise of tide over Crow Bar when heading for St Mary's Pool around the N of the island.

St Mary's Road

This anchorage lies near the centre of the group of islands and is the main anchorage for visiting cruise liners and other larger vessels in depths of up to 15m. It is available as an anchorage for yachts and smaller vessels in winds from NW-N-NE-E but it becomes very uncomfortable with any swell from the SE-S-

SW-W and dangerous under SW gale conditions when even large ships may have to seek shelter in the lee of St Mary's Island (see Hats SE and NW below). Yachts can also find shelter in Porth Cressa or New Grimsby Sound.

Leading marks

Line P
St Martin's daymark on summit of Creeb on 041° clears Woodcock Ledge

Warning In the event of SW or W winds yachts should leave this anchorage and proceed to New Grimsby Sound or to Crow Sound. A network of cables crosses between St Mary's and Tresco in the area of Crow Bar and between the larger islands (see plan pages 22–23).

Hats SE and NW

Sheltered S-SW-W-NW-N. The deep water anchorages used by large vessels when there is a SW gale. Anchor in 5–12m sand 400m to SE and also 1,000m to NW of Hats yellow and black S cardinal buoy, ⚑ topmark (VQ(6)+LFl.10s).

Tidal streams

In St Mary's Road stream begins:

Local HW	Devonport HW	Dover HW	Direction	Max rate knots		Remarks
				Springs	Neaps	
–0550	+0540	+0015	E	1	–	Constant direction
–0050	–0145	+0515	SW–W–NW	¾	–	Direction varies

MINOR ANCHORAGES

Old Town Bay
⊕ 49°54'.6N 06°18'.00W

Sheltered SW-W-NW-N-NE. The original harbour for St Mary's which dries. The inner part of the bay (inside Carn Leh) is now fully occupied with moorings leased to the Old Town Boat Club and there is no longer space to anchor. Some shelter may be found in the outer part of the bay but even here the entrance requires great care owing to dangers on either hand. This was the original port for St Mary's but is now a small village with two cafés, Old Town Café and Tolman Licenced Café (☎ 01720 423060). The Old Town Inn (☎ 01720 422301), open 1100–2230, offers bar and bistro meals (open all day from 1200) and Old Town Stores (☎ 01720 423300) is an off-licence as well as selling provisions. There is a church at the head of the bay and the airport control tower is ¼M to E. The W side of the head of the harbour is foul and there is an old quay and slip on the E side.

Porth Hellick and Porth Loggos
⊕ 49°54'.90N 06°17'.00W
⊕ 49°54'.75N 06°16'.88W

Sheltered SW-W-NW-N-NE. Port Hellick is a drying anchorage, difficult to enter and only suitable for small craft. It is relatively deserted but there can be a heavy and dangerous swell in onshore winds. Only enter in good conditions, on a NW heading from Porth Hellick Point. Sir Cloudesley Shovell's memorial and a Bronze Age burial chamber are nearby (see photo page 39). Although Sir Cloudesley Shovell was originally buried here after his body was washed ashore he was later reburied in Westminster Abbey. The beach is famous for its shells. An alternative but exposed anchorage is in Porth Loggos, just W of Newfoundland Point in 6m rocks and sand.

Pendrathen
⊕ 49°56'.10N 06°18.10W

Sheltered E-SE-S-SW-W. A drying anchorage, easy to enter on a SE heading and used as a small craft mooring area. Wras, a rocky patch

St Mary's.
Porth Cressa (L),
Peninnis head and
Old Town Bay (R),
Hugh Town
beyond
Patrick Roach

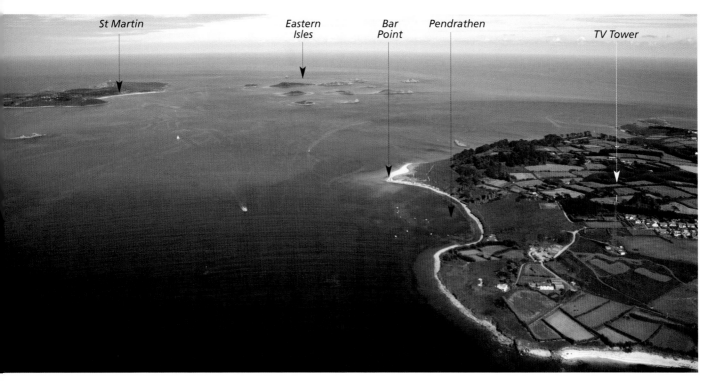

St Martin   Eastern Isles   Bar Point   Pendrathen   TV Tower

View NE over Pendrathen and Bar Point, St Mary's to St Martin's and Eastern Isles
Patrick Roach

Porthloo and Taylor's Island, St Mary's

(dries 5m) in the centre of the bay, is marked by a pole. There is a cable beacon with yellow ⧫ topmark at Bar Point and a ruined jetty at the opposite end of the small bay.

Toll's Porth
⊕ 49°55.80N 06°18'.50W

Sheltered NE-E-SE. A small drying anchorage with a rocky bottom. Halangy Down Settlement, an Iron age village and Bant's Carn, a Bronze age burial chamber, maintained by English heritage are nearby ashore.

Porth Loo
49°55'.30N 06°18'.50W

A large drying anchorage with sand and rock bottom, easy to enter on an E heading. A boatyard capable of hauling and repairing wooden boats with a draft of up to 2m and a small collection of houses ashore. Juliet's Garden (☎01720 422228) restaurant and tearoom overlooks the bay.

View from Porth Loo across Newford Island to St Mary's Pool

FACILITIES

Moorings
41 in St Mary's Pool.

Landing places
Visitors' dinghy pontoon clearly marked below the steps at the junction of New Quay and Old Quay. Visitors' tenders should be moored between second and third pontoons. Do not use the main quay or steps along it because of constant traffic from *Scillonian III*, inter-island ferries, and service or cargo vessels. Tenders can also be left on Town Beach, Porth Mellon Beach and on the beach at Porth Cressa.

Harbourmaster
Captain Glen Covell. Harbour office next to hotel on the quay, open daily 0800–1900. VHF Ch.16 (Working Ch.14).
Harbour Office, The Quay, Hugh Town, St Mary's, Isles of Scilly, TR21 0HU.
☎ 01720 422768 (07789 273626 out of hours).
Fax 01720 423980.
Email hm@stmarys-harbour.co.uk www.stmarys-harbour.co.uk

Police
Police station, Garrison Lane, Hugh Town.
☎ 01720 422444 or 08452 777444 for immediate attention.

Chandlery
Southard Engineering, Thorofare, Hughtown ☎ 01720 422539.

Marine Engineers
Nike Engineering, Porth Mellon ☎ 01720 422991.
Southard Engineering ☎ 01720 422539.

Boat repairs
Peter Martin ☎ 01720 422972 or 07775 717052.
Isles of Scilly Steamship Company ☎ 01720 422710.

Sailmakers
Rat Island Sail Locker (Keith Buchanan) ☎ 01720 422037 or 423399 keith@ratisland.net

Weather
A local weather bulletin is posted daily outside the Harbour Office at 0830 (GMT) and also at the Tourist Information Centre, Porth Cressa.

Internet
A computer with internet access is available in the harbourmaster's office – £1 for 15 minutes. Harbour area covered by Wi-Fi hotspot system. Internet access also available at several hotels and cafés by arrangement including Woodcock & Mumford's Deli (£1 for ½ hour), the library, Tourist Information Centre, The airport, Tregarthen's Hotel, The Boatshed and the Longstone Centre.

Divers
Mark Groves ☎ 01720 422732 or 07747 615732 www.islandseasafaris.co.uk, Dave McBride ☎ 01720 422455, Scavenger Diving ☎ 01720 423420.

Water
Larger amounts are available (metered) direct to vessels alongside the quay by prior arrangement with the harbourmaster. Containers may also be filled from a tap near to the harbour office with the harbourmaster's permission.

Fuel
Sibleys Fuel & Marine Services, Rat Island, Hugh Town. ☎ 01720 422431 or 07810 301050 www.sibleysonscilly.com. Open 0800–0930, 1030–1130 and 1300–1700. New in 2010 are diesel and petrol pumps on the quay. Also available in cans from fuel stations on Telegraph Road and at Porth Cressa.

Gas
Camping gaz and Flogas from Sibleys (see Fuel above). Calor Gas from Island Home Hardware, Garrison Lane, Hugh Town ☎ 01720 422388.

Refuse
Recycling scheme on the islands. Skips on the quay close to the dinghy pontoon. Litter bins at Porth Cressa.

Showers & WCs
Coin operated showers and WCs next to the harbour office and open 24 hours. Public toilets at Porth Cressa and in Lower Strand.

Telephones
Mobile reception on St Mary's is variable. Coin and card operated 'phones are to be found behind the harbour office, in the Harbourside Hotel on the quay, at the foot of Garrison Hill and in The Parade, Hugh Town.

Post Office
Hugh St, Hugh Town.(☎ 01720 422454) Open 0815–1630 Monday to Friday and 0815–1215 on Saturday. Post box on the quay. Harbourmaster will also keep mail, send and receive Faxes.

Banks
Lloyds TSB ☎ 01720 422418 and Barclays ☎ 0845 7555555, both in Hugh Street, open 0900–1630 Monday to Friday. Cash point at Lloyds TSB. Cashback facilities in the Coop and R Douglas (Chemist). Some cards and cheques can be used to obtain cash at Post Offices.

Shops
Hugh Town has a broad selection of shops. Coop Supermarket open 0800–2200 and 0800–1600 on Sundays. Butcher/baker (☎ 01720 422626), fishmonger, greengrocer, delicatessen, R Douglas, pharmacy (☎ 01720 422403), Mumfords, newsagent, clothes and gift shops, mostly open 0900–1700 with half day closing on Wednesday out of season.

Launderette
At Porth Cressa, open 0900–1700 Monday to Saturday.

Restaurants
There is a wide selection of pubs, cafés, takeaways, hotels and restaurants in Hugh Town including: Atlantic Inn (☎ 01720 422417), Bishop & Wolf (☎ 01720 422771), Blues Restaurant (☎ 01720 422221), The Boatshed, Porth Mellon (☎ 01720 423881 or 07748 805273), Chez Michel (☎ 01720 422871), The Deli, Woodcock & Mumford, The

Town Beach, Hugh Town, St Mary's
David Lomax

Galley (✆ 01720 422602), Juliet's Garden (✆ 01720 422228), The Mermaid (✆ 01720 422701), Pilot Gig (✆ 01720 422654 or 423279), Star Castle Hotel (✆ 01720 422317), Tregarthen's Hotel (✆ 01720 422540). In Old Town: Old Town Inn (✆ 01720 422301).

Medical

Health Clinic and Hospital, Hospital Lane (off Church Street) ✆ 01720 422392. Doctor (health centre) and pharmacy ✆ 01720 422628. Dentist ✆ 01720 422694. Chemist R Douglas ✆ 01720 422403.

Transport

Taxis: Island Taxis (✆ 01720 422126 or 422635), St Mary's Taxis (✆ 01720 422555), Scilly Cabs (✆ 01720 422901) and Q Cabs (✆ 01720 422260), buses (including island tours) and Car Hire. Bicycle rental at St Mary's Bike Hire, The Strand (✆ 0779 6638506).

Tourist Information Centre

Porth Cressa, open Monday to Saturday (✆ 01720 424031 www.simplyscilly.co.uk).

Churches

Church of England, Methodist and Roman Catholic churches in Hugh Town. Yacht deliveries – Sibleys (see Fuel above).

Ferries

Regular launches to off-islands from the quay. St Mary's Boatmen's Association ✆ 01720 423999 or Bryher Boat Services ✆ 01720 422886. Information about pleasure trips at Old Quay. Mainland links Isles of Scilly Skybus (✆ 01720 422905 www.ios-travel.co.uk). British International Helicopters (✆ 01720 422646 www.islesofscillyhelicopter.com) and *MV Scillonian III* Isles of Scilly Steamship Company (✆ 01720 422357 www.ios-travel.co.uk).

Attractions

St Mary's museum, Church Street, Hugh Town (✆ 01720 422337). Gig racing on Wednesday and Friday evenings, finishing at the end of the quay. Wildlife tours. Guided walks. Bird watching. Natural History tours. (Information available at Tourist Information Centre). Bird watching, Isles of Scilly Wildlife Trust (✆ 01720 422153 www.ios-wildlifetrust.org.uk), Isles of Scilly Bird Group (www.scillybirding.co.uk). Scilly walks, archaeological and historical walks. (✆ 01720 423326 www.scillywalks.co.uk). Island Sea Safaris (✆ 01720 422732 or 07747 1015732).

HISTORY AND VISITS ASHORE

St Mary's forms the hub for the islands and Hugh Town is the administrative capital of Scilly, the commercial centre and the port for connections to both the mainland and the off-islands. The airport on the E side if the island provides the main air link with the mainland although there are direct helicopter links to Tresco. The quay in Hugh Town is a hive of activity in the daytime with the coming and going of inter-island boats, tripper boats on expeditions to look at lighthouses, birds or seals and service craft of many varieties. The topography of Scilly means that the doctor and midwife, the ambulance service and goods delivery services all have their own craft, as do the harbourmaster, the pilot and the diver. The St Mary's Boatmen's Association (✆ 01720 423999) was founded in 1958 by island boatmen with craft, mostly owned and operated by the same families for many years. There are a number of other independent operators, notably Bryher Boat Services (✆ 01720 422886) who operate powerful water jet powered RIBs.

Hugh Town takes its name from the 'hugh' or 'hoe' on which it is situated, meaning a promontory or, in this case, a narrow sandbar, dividing Porth Cressa from St Mary's Pool. The harbour is privately run by the Duchy of Cornwall which has owned the Isles of Scilly since 1337, although most of the houses in Hugh Town are now in private ownership. Originally known as Ennor, St Mary's had its first capital at Old Town in the S of the island with a nearby castle dating from the thirteenth century. In the reign of Elizabeth I the focus began to shift to Hugh Town and the Queen ordered the construction of a new fortification on Garrison Hill to serve as a defence against Spain and protection from privateers. This fortress, in the shape of an eight-pointed star, was completed in 1583–4 and was followed by the building of the harbour quay in 1601. This was subsequently extended to Rat Island and further to seaward in the nineteenth century, allowing access at all states of the tide and forming a more effective breakwater.

St Mary's also has the highest land in the archipelago at Telegraph (48m) on the NW side, marked by the 15m-high, grey, round stone telegraph tower. Close to this are a latticed grey mobile telephone mast and a communications aerial. To the NNW, is the tall, latticework TV tower, prominent because of its height (119m) throughout Scilly when the visibility is good. The mast and control tower of the airport are noticeable. The lighthouse at the S tip, on Pendennis Head, is small, not very prominent and can easily be confused with the old St Agnes light when approaching from the E. In the approach to St Mary's Pool the round stone Buzza Tower (37m) is prominent as is the nearby white generator chimney (48m).

Star Castle, looking S from St Mary's Road

St Mary's Pool with Rat Island and New Quay in the foreground and Newford Island beyond

Star Castle is an important landmark, though not always an obvious one from seaward, and its ramparts afford a fine all-round view of the islands. Built by Francis Godolphin in 1583, it was a Royalist stronghold during the Civil War and a staging-post for the future Charles II in 1646 on his way to exile in France. The Royalists, led by Sir John Grenville, controlled the castle and the surrounding seas for three years; they were finally forced to surrender in 1651, when Parliamentarian forces under Admiral Blake landed on Tresco and imposed a blockade. The garrison walls, batteries, guard-house, barracks, magazine and prison were built between 1715 and 1746 but the military establishment was gradually reduced. Star Castle and the surrounding fortifications are carefully preserved although the castle itself has been a hotel since 1933.

Woolpack Beacon from St Mary's with Gugh in the background

Hugh Town today is a real little town, the only one in Scilly, with many facilities and much activity, particularly when the ferry arrives from the mainland. A weekly service to the mainland was started in the early nineteenth century by the Tregarthen brothers, owners of the hotel of that name. In 1920, the islanders founded the Isles of Scilly Steamship Company and the first *Scillonian*, carrying passengers, cargo and mail, was launched soon afterwards. In those days, when a permanent watch was kept at the coastguard station on Telegraph, a black ball would be hoisted up the mast, to indicate that the ferry had left the mainland; the ball was dropped when she came into sight, thus warning the local taxi drivers, hoteliers and shopkeepers to prepare for visitors. The present *Scillonian III* was commissioned in 1977, while the *Gry Maritha* was purchased in 1989 to handle additional freight.

Although sometimes overshadowed by the attractions of the other islands, St Mary's has its own special charm, a fact no doubt appreciated by the former prime minister Harold Wilson,

Hugh Town, St Mary's

A new gig in build by Peter Martin at Porth Loo

who made his holiday home here in the 1960s. Heathery downs, marshes and pools, lush valleys and woods, bulb fields enclosed by hedges, pretty coves and beaches – all compose a varied landscape, and one that is easily explored on foot.

The racing of pilot gigs originated on Scilly and the world championships are held there every year. These elegant boats are long, fast, clinker built skiffs about 10m long with six oars and competition amongst the crews is fierce. Originally, before the advent of steam ships, crews would race out to meet ships and put a pilot aboard but they were also used for lifesaving and rescue purposes, saving many lives from ships wrecked on the treacherous rocks around the islands. Originally designed to sail (The *Klondyke* in the museum is exhibited with her sails) in suitable weather, the gigs are now raced competitively in many ports around the UK and in a growing number of other countries. There are now over 100 of these beautiful craft and, for every club, or seaside village with a gig there is not only a top crew but also a ladies crew, a junior crew, a veterans crew and more; they have become a hugely

Pilot gig *Klondyke* built in 1873 and now exhibited in the museum, St Mary's

successful community sport. Gigs are still built regularly on the islands but some of the very early craft built over 150 years ago are still rowed competitively.

Peninnis Head, reached by the coastal path, provides a stark contrast to this otherwise gentle scene. The cliffs and rocks have been carved by the weather into weird shapes, which have been given fanciful names such as Tooth Rock and Laughing Man. In geological terms, they are excellent examples of the vertical and horizontal decomposition of granite. The automatic Peninnis light is an unusual-looking structure on a latticework support but it is a vital aid to navigation installed in 1911.

For lovers of history, St Mary's has several important ancient sites, many of them well maintained by English Heritage. At Halangy Down, on the NW coast near Telegraph, is a village of round houses, which date from about the second century BC and was still in use in Roman times. S of the settlement is the 3,000 year old burial chamber at Bant's Carn, thought to have been an ancestral shrine. (The location of Bant's Carn is correctly shown on the Ordnance Survey map, but incorrectly on the Admiralty chart where it is shown at Bant's Carn Battery to N).

Further tombs are to be found at Innisidgen, on the other side of Telegraph, at Porth Hellick Down, on the E shore, and on Buzza Hill, above Hugh Town. The squat Buzza Tower, which is a reference mark when approaching St Mary's harbour from the sea, was originally a Martello tower and later a windmill. The tower on Telegraph was also constructed against a possible French invasion. In 1814, it acquired a semaphore, for sending signals to the mainland. This was the only direct means of communication until, in 1902, as a result of experiments conducted there by Marconi, a radio mast was erected and a coastguard station established, one of the earliest to be equipped with wireless telegraphy. Harry's Walls above the beach at Porth Mellon was a small artillery fort of Italianate and, for its date, advanced design. Construction commenced in 1551 but unfortunately the design was flawed and it was never completed. Within the walls are an old granite day mark and the more recent higher transit mark for the entrance to St Mary's Pool.

The E coast of St Mary's is designated a Special Area within the Isles of Scilly Marine Park, on account of its sponges, corals and sea fans, which are not only rare but slow growing and easily damaged. Watermill Cove is a delightful little anchorage, well sheltered from the SW and with a sandy beach at LW. In the eighteenth century, it had a quay for the export of kelp, the product of burning seaweed, which was done in pits on Toll's Island. Pelistry Bay is a popular picnic spot with a large, secluded beach, although currents make swimming hazardous when the bar between island and shore is covered.

Peninnis Head and lighthouse, St Mary's

Memorial to Sir Cloudesley Shovell at Porth Hollick,
St Mary's

Bronze Age entrance grave Bant's Carn, St Mary's

Porth Hollick, to the south, is the bay where the body of Sir Cloudesley Shovell was washed ashore in 1707 (see photo above). A rough-hewn monument commemorates the event. If one continues past the airport, completed at the beginning of the second world war to replace the landing strip on the golf course, one reaches Old Town. The Church there is the remnant of a much larger, Norman edifice and was renovated in 1891. By then, however, it had been superseded by the new church in Hugh Town, built in 1838, which Augustus Smith was required to provide under the terms of his lease as Lord Proprietor. In Old Town churchyard are buried over a hundred victims of another famous wreck, the *Schiller*, which foundered in 1875.

The road leads directly back to Hugh Town, conveniently passing the excellent museum which houses many interesting marine artefacts, ancient tools, pottery and jewellery recovered from burial chambers on the islands and examples of the many rare birds and other wildlife found around Scilly. A diversion can be taken to Porth Cressa, which is a useful alternative anchorage to St Mary's Pool, especially in a NW wind. This, together with Town Beach opposite, was once the centre of the shipbuilding industry, which enjoyed a brief boom with the encouragement of Augustus Smith. By the 1850s, there were four yards at work, but thirty years later they had all closed, unable to cope with the latest technology of iron, steam-driven vessels.

Old Grimsby Sound, Tresco with Bryher beyond and Norwethel (right)
Patrick Roach

Tresco, Bryher and Samson

OVERVIEW

Tresco

The island of Tresco is the second largest in Scilly after St Mary's ; it is about two miles long, half a mile across and covers an area of 297 hectares. The southern shore of Tresco is just a mile from St Mary's. The permanent population is approximately 130, much augmented by a regular influx of visitors throughout the year, staying in the hotel, inn or the growing number of holiday cottages. The whole island is a private estate, leased from the Duchy of Cornwall by the Dorrien-Smith family, descendants of the great Augustus Smith who did so much for the islands in the nineteenth century. The island is well provided with an excellent shop and other facilities for the holidaymakers and is renowned for the world famous Tresco Abbey gardens.

Bryher

Bryher (pronounced 'briar') measures one and a half miles long by roughly half a mile wide and is the smallest of the inhabited islands. It lies just to the W of Tresco, divided from it by New Grimsby Sound, and is about 2–3 M from St Mary's. The total area, including the deserted islet of Gweal which lies close offshore to W is 133 hectares and the permanent population is about 65. Bryher takes its namefrom the Celtic for 'big' and 'hill' and is relatively elevated for an island in such a notoriously low archipelago as Scilly. Watch Hill (43m), with its stone

Porth Bryher looking N with Great Par and Hell Bay Hotel in the foreground
Patrick Roach

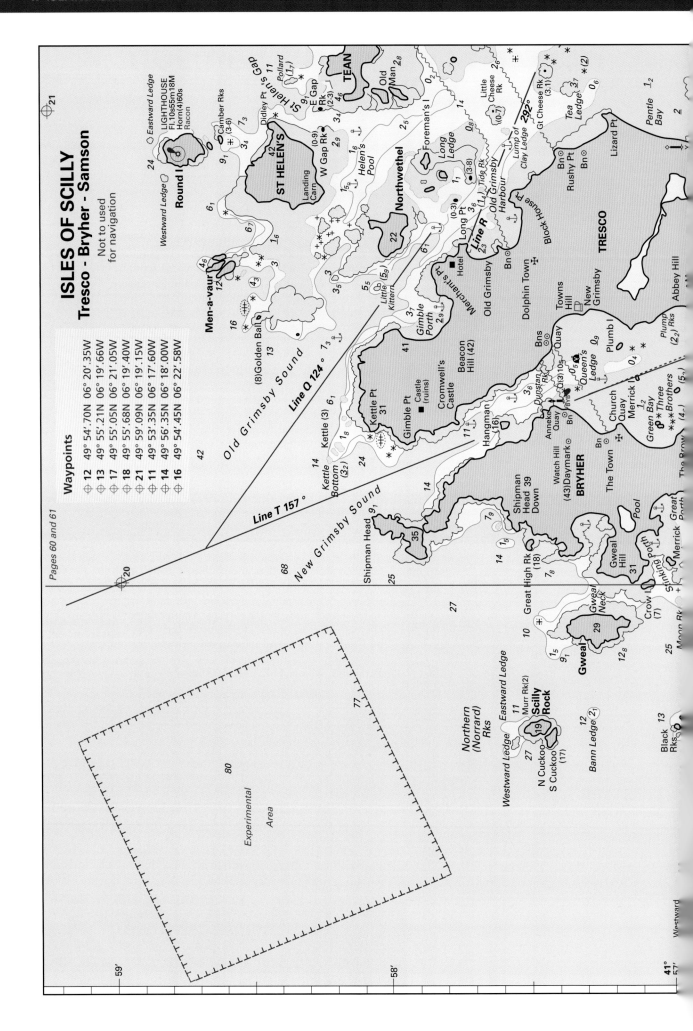

ISLES OF SCILLY
Tresco - Bryher - Samson

Not to used
for navigation

Waypoints

⊕ 12	49°54'.70N	06°20'.35W
⊕ 13	49°55'.21N	06°19'.66W
⊕ 17	49°55'.05N	06°21'.05W
⊕ 18	49°55'.68N	06°19'.40W
⊕ 21	49°59'.09N	06°19'.15W
⊕ 11	49°53'.35N	06°17'.60W
⊕ 14	49°56'.35N	06°18'.00W
⊕ 16	49°54'.45N	06°22'.58W

Pages 60 and 61

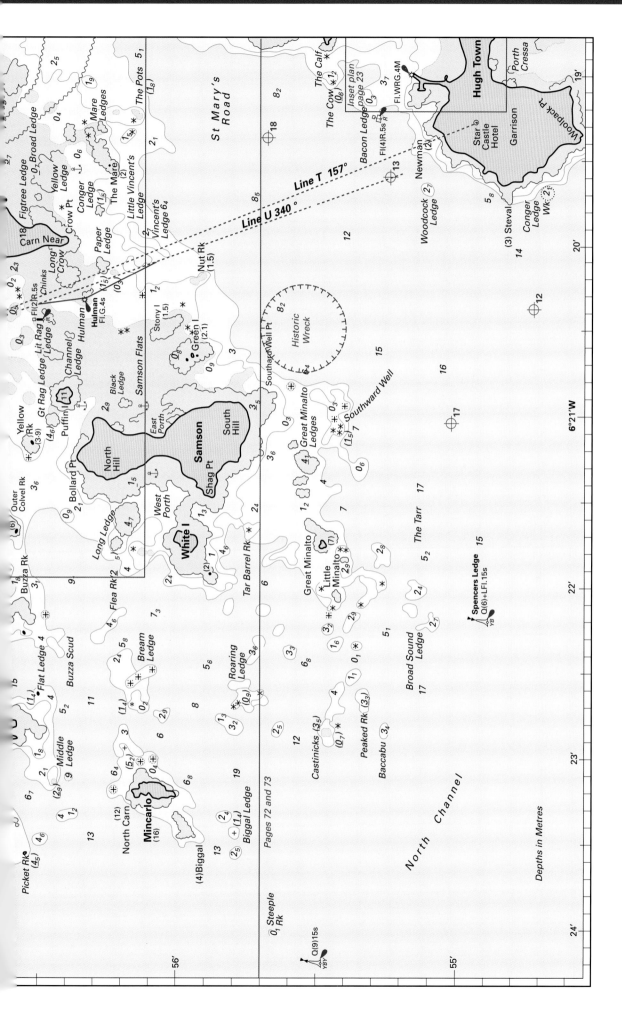

South Hill   Castle Bryher   North Hill   Scilly Rock   Gweal

Samson, looking NW from Star Castle Hotel (St Mary's)

daymark, the flatter Shipman Head Down (39m) to the N , and the rounded Samson Hill (40m) at the S end are all distinctive features useful for navigation. So too is the pyramidal Hangman Island off the NE coast which is easy to recognise in the approaches to New Grimsby Sound – especially when it has gallows on top!

Samson

Samson is just over half a mile long, a third of a mile wide at its broadest, 39 hectares in area, and less than ½M S of Bryher. At one time there were 34 residents on the island but numbers dwindled and, since 1855, the island has been unoccupied. The twin rounded hills (33m and 40m), joined by a low, sandy isthmus, are unmistakeable landmarks from most directions.

Men-a-vaur, Golden Ball Brow and Round Island from N Tresco

PASSAGES

In settled weather the easiest approaches to Tresco, Bryher and Samson are from the north (see pages 42 and 43) but these should not be contemplated in strong winds or poor visibility. The only significant light in the area is on Round Island and wind over tide can produce overfalls in the whole area of approach. New Grimsby Sound divides Tresco from Bryher with visitors' moorings and an anchorage which offer some of the best shelter in the archipelago although it is open to the N and the swell can be uncomfortable in strong winds from NW and SW. At an appropriate state of the tide, the sound provides a passage through to Samson and St Mary's Road although great care needs to be taken when calculating tidal depth as most of this area dries at LW. The prudent yachtsman will only undertake this passage on a rising tide! Old Grimsby Sound gives access to the anchorage at Old Grimsby on the East side of Tresco but the warnings apply equally to this passage.

Tidal streams

NW of Bryher:

Local HW	Plymouth HW	Dover HW	Direction	Rate (knots) Spring	Neaps
-0505	-0600	+0045	WSW	1.0	0.5
-0205	-0300	+0345	ENE	1.6	0.8
+0055	0000	-0540	ENE	0.9	0.5
+0355	+0300	-0240	SW	1.3	0.6
+0555	+0600	+0020	WSW	1.2	0.6

Note: Stream reaches 1.9 knots at HW Plymouth -2H in springs.

New Grimsby Sound

Buoys and beacons

The Bar
East cardinal beacon, yellow and black with ◆ topmark. Q(3)10s. 60m NE The Bar, Bryher – almost opposite New Grimsby harbour

Little Rag Ledge
Red beacon with radar reflector topmark Fl(2)R.5s on a small rock which dries

Hulman
Pole beacon with green ▲ topmark Fl.G.4s on a small rock which dries

Little Rag Ledge beacon looking W to Castle Bryher

Hulman beacon with Samson (left) and Puffin Island (right) in the background

New Grimsby Sound looking N with Bryher (left) and Tresco (right)
Patrick Roach

Church Quay   Shipman Head   Hangman Island   Cromwell's Castle   New Grimsby Quay

Entrance to New Grimsby Sound on a calm day with Cromwell's Castle (left), Hangman Island (Centre) and Shipman Head (right) *Le Page / Anderson*

Leading marks

Line T

W side Hangman Island on Star Castle Hotel on St Mary's on 157° leads into New Grimsby Sound from ⊕ 20

Line U

Merrick Island on Hangman Island on 340° (stern transit) leads over Tresco Flats

Warning

Strong cross-tidal streams exist in the approach and must be allowed for. (*See table below*). Overfalls occur over Kettle Bottom which lies off N Tresco between Old and New Grimsby Sounds.

Directions

New Grimsby Sound leads into the gap between Tresco to E and Bryher to W and is, arguably, the easiest entry of the four main anchorages in Scilly. Yachtsmen making directly for New Grimsby Sound from the mainland should set a course that will take them well N of Round Island, clearing the Islets and rocks N of White Island and St Martin's. The passage should be planned for a daytime arrival as there are no lit marks in the area apart from Round Island. Once Round Island is abeam then a course should be set to ⊕ 20 which lies on transit line T for New Grimsby Sound. The transit can be seen from well to seaward in clear visibility, formed by the right hand side of Hangman Island with the prominent building, The Star Castle Hotel on Garrison Hill – the westernmost part of St Mary's – on a bearing of 157°. This

transit leads clear of all the dangerous rocks on the port hand side of the sound and, once a yacht is abeam of Cromwell's Castle, the anchorage, which is largely filled with visitors' moorings, will be clearly visible and accessible. If the above transit is not easily seen, but you are nonetheless sure of your position outside the entrance to the sound, then Shipman Head to starboard is quite steep-to and there are no off-lying rocks or obstructions on this side of the channel. By approaching to within 100m of the shore, close under the lee of Shipman Head, you can quickly avoid the worst of the Atlantic swell and move out of the path of any wind from W or SW. At the same time you will be able to steer well clear of the rocks called Kettle and Kettle Bottom which extend north-westwards from the main island of Tresco. From under Shipman Head steer towards Cromwell's Castle – the only building to be seen at that point on the Tresco shoreline. From a mid-point in the sound the visitors' moorings will open up and a course should be shaped slightly to starboard to lay the anchorage, passing equidistant from Hangman to starboard and Tresco to port. As one enters the sound, the most obvious feature is undoubtedly the pyramid-shaped 16m high Hangman Island which stands almost in the middle of the sound and is joined to Bryher at low water.

When there is enough water the passage S over Tresco Flats to St Mary's Road can be undertaken but as much of this area dries at LAT it should only be contemplated after careful planning and preferably on a rising tide. Leave the moorings in New Grimsby on a S course, passing Plumb Island 100m to port and then Merrick Island 100m to starboard, keeping close enough to Merrick Island to clear Plump Rocks on the Tresco side of the channel. Tresco's harbourmaster has provided two white pole leading marks to the S of Plumb Hill which mark the N side of the sandbank and rocks running SW from Appletree Point (See photo page 47). The lower mark has two flashing solar lights and the upper a single flashing solar light. When Merrick is 300m astern steer 160° with stern transit of Merrick on Hangman 340° (line U). Leave Little Rag Ledge beacon (Fl(2)R.5s) 50m to starboard and Hulman beacon (Fl.G.4s) 50m to port. Then leave Nut Rock 50m to starboard and pass into St Mary's Road.

Tidal streams

In New Grimsby Sound:

Local HW	Plymouth HW	Dover HW	Direction	Remarks
-0505	-0600	+0045	SE	*Stream changes*
-0205	-0300	+0345	NW	*direction four times*
+0055	0000	-0540	SE	*in 12 hours*
0355	+0300	-0240	NW	
+0555	+0600	+0020	Slack	

New Grimsby Harbour (Tresco)   Hangman I.   Star Castle Hotel (St Mary's)   Bryher

Entrance from N into New Grimsby Sound, with visitors' moorings (left), looking SSE;
W edge of Hangman I. on Star Castle Hotel (St Mary's) on 157° (line T)

Bryher   Merrick I. Hangman I.   Carn Near (Tresco)   Tresco Abbey

Looking NW from Star Castle Hotel (St Mary's) at LW; Hangman I. with
Merrick I. on 340° is the stern transit (line U) leading over Tresco Flats

Shipman Head   Hangman Island   Cromwell's Castle   Leading Mark

Looking NW from Appletree Point, Tresco

Harbourmaster's leading marks, Tresco
Mike Lewin-Harris

View NW between Samson and Bryher from leading
marks on Tresco

Old Grimsby Sound

Leading Marks

Line Q
Rock 3.8m high between Merchant's Point and SW side Northwethel leads through the entrance to Old Grimsby Sound on 124° (see photo below)

Line R
Island Hotel on Long Point Slip leads away SE from Old Grimsby Harbour clear of Blockhouse Point on 292° (stern transit)

Line S
Crow Rock beacon on TV tower (160°31') leads towards St Mary's Road (see photo page 49)

Warning
Strong cross-tidal streams exist off the N entrance to the sound (see table page 45) and must be allowed for. Overfalls exist over Kettle Bottom off the point between Old and New Grimsby Sounds and can occur across the entrance to the sound between Kettle Bottom and Golden Ball Brow.

Directions
Providing the weather is fair approach the entrance to Old Grimsby Sound from the general direction of ⊕20, leaving the Tresco shore under Tregarthen Hill about 100m to starboard. Positively identify Norwethel Island (22m) on the NE side of Old Grimsby Sound as you enter. Although the entrance to Old Grimsby Sound shows depths between 11m at the entrance and 3.3m off Old Grimsby Harbour there is a drying rock called Little Kittern (dries 1.9m) close abeam, to port of the

Entrance to Old Grimsby Sound from N

Old Grimsby and approaches looking N
Patrick Roach

fairway in the approach. As Gimble Porth opens up to starboard head for the middle of the gap between Norwethel to port and Merchant's Point to starboard. At this point the features of the line of bearing (line Q) should, if recognised, be followed. Trafford Rock at the rear of Old Grimsby harbour is charted on Admiralty Chart 883 at 3.8m high, about 300m NNE of Block House Point, Tresco. Close this rock on 122° and this achieves a safe arrival in the moorings of Old Grimsby. If in doubt and if time is available it is a good idea to stand at Block House Point at low water when both the 3.8m charted rock and the, particularly dangerous, charted Tide Rock (dries 1.4m) will be apparent. Tide Rock lies about 100m inshore of the 3.8m rock. If not then the line of permanent red visitors' moorings ahead can be approached directly from the middle of the gap mentioned above. Despite these mooring buoys there is room to anchor, both NW and SE of them.

When there is sufficient height of tide then yachts may head S to St Mary's Road or Crow Sound from the moorings in Old Grimsby Sound. Set a course to clear Block House Point with a stern transit of 292°, Island Hotel on Long Point Slip (Line R), to clear just 50m S of Tide Rock (dries 1.1m) and Lump of Clay Ledge (dries 1.4m). Off Rushy Point, Tresco bring Crow Rock beacon onto the TV Tower (St Mary's) on 160° (Line S) and this leads in to St Mary's Road although this course crosses sand and rocky patches which dry 0.7m.

New Grimsby at LW with Bryher beyond
Mike Lewin-Harris

MAIN ANCHORAGES AND MOORINGS

New Grimsby Sound, Tresco & Bryher

Sheltered N-NE-E-SE-S-SW-W. The approach is described in 'Passages' (Page 45). At HW the anchorage can become uncomfortable with strong S – SSW winds and swell and can become rough with strong NW winds and swell.

The anchorage lies on a NW/SE line between Hangman Island and Frenchman's Point to the NW and a line joining the yellow mark NW of New Grimsby Harbour quay and the smaller yellow mark on the shore under Watch Hill, Bryher. These two yellow marks show where not to anchor owing to buried transmission lines. There is an E cardinal beacon (with ♦ topmark, Q(3)10s) at the end of Anneka's Quay just E of Watch Hill on Bryher. Depths in the anchorage vary from about 5m in the NW to about 2m in the SE. The bottom is sand and gravel. At Springs the tide runs at 2 knots or more. In addition to the fishing boat and local moorings on the Bryher side of the channel there are 24 red and yellow visitors' mooring buoys laid in the anchorage on the Tresco side. Call Henry Birch, the helpful harbourmaster, on VHF Ch.16 or on ☎01720 422792 or mobile ☎07778 601237. Most of the moorings are suitable for yachts of up to 40′ but the two outer moorings are suitable for vessels of up to 60′ and 80′. The moorings somewhat restrict the space available for fin-keel vessels to anchor but, with care, space can be found in the westerly part of the anchorage. The fee for

Looking on a bearing of 160° on the transit of Crow Rock beacon with the TV Tower, St Mary's (Line S)

Tidal streams

In Old Grimsby Sound:

Local HW	Plymouth HW	Dover HW	Direction	Remarks
-0505	-0600	+0045	SE	SE stream runs 8 hours
-0205	-0300	+0345	SE	
+0055	0000	-0540	SE	
+0355	+0300	-0240	NW	NW stream runs 4 hours
+0555	+0600	-0020	SE	

anchoring was £10 (2009), the overnight charge for a visitor's mooring was £20 or £30 for larger boats. If two nights are paid for then the third night is free. Fees are collected by the Tresco harbourmaster Henry Birch but if you plan an early departure please pay the day beforehand or leave appropriate payment at the Estate Office. The visitors' moorings are heavy-duty and, except in the dirtiest weather conditions, offer reliable security to properly moored vessels. Visitors must supply their own mooring strops for these buoys and in strong NW winds would be wise to back up rope strops with chain strops and shackles. One problem in this anchorage is the extensive Japanese seaweed which is particularly rife at low water. If using the engine to charge batteries, weed can entirely block the engine cooling water intake. Check the exhaust when charging! There is reasonable dinghy access to Tresco, with sufficient rise of tide, anywhere on the shore within New Grimsby Harbour. As in all Scilly harbours, visitors' dinghies are not allowed to be secured alongside the protective quay which is used by ferries and commercial vessels. There is room for one medium-size yacht to dry out alongside the inshore part of the harbour quay provided permission has been granted by the harbourmaster. In the season the seaward end of the quay is extremely busy with tourist traffic during daylight hours. New Grimsby harbour dries, is full of private moorings and is not open to visiting yachts, even if they can take the ground. New Grimsby anchorage also gives convenient access to Bryher. At high water, ferries use the stone quay close to Bryher church but at other times they use the recently upgraded low water quay extending from The Bar opposite New Grimsby quay. This is the most convenient dinghy landing point but dinghies should not be secured in such a way as to obstruct ferry access. This quay, known as 'Anneka's Quay' was built originally as a project in the *Challenge Anneka* TV programme series and has recently been extended and improved by the Duchy of Cornwall.

Old Grimsby Harbour (Tresco)

Some shelter is given from wind in all directions. The anchorage lies between an imaginary line between the charted Island Hotel with the S end of Norwethel and a point about 150m NE of Blockhouse Point marking the SE end of the harbour. Within this area there are six red and yellow visitors' moorings for which overnight charges are payable to the Tresco harbourmaster (charges are the same as at New Grimsby) or, in his absence, to the Island Hotel. There is, however, a fair amount of room for fin-keel yachts to anchor within the suggested boundaries and there is still water to about 2.5m depth SE of Tide Rock. The bottom is mainly sand and gravel. SE of Tide Rock anchors need to be set with care. If in doubt re-anchor with sufficient scope until you are happy. At Springs the tide can run at over 2 knots. Ashore the Island Hotel has an excellent restaurant but booking is advisable. The hotel is due to be demolished and re-built at the end of the 2010 season.

Old Grimsby at LW
Le Page / Anderson

MINOR ANCHORAGES

Rushy Porth (Tresco)

49°57'.25N 06°19.25W

Sheltered S-SW-W-NW-N-NE. A drying anchorage off the beach. Approach by old Grimsby Sound (see page 48). The amount of shelter depends on the height of tide but the bay is usually deserted. The bay is full of rocks and boulders and yachts intending to take the ground should only do so with great care. Cables run ashore near the centre of the bay and at Rushy Point where there are beacons with yellow ♦ topmarks.

Green Porth & Ravens Porth, Old Grimsby (Tresco)

These two porths are separated by a projecting quay and together form Old Grimsby harbour. Approach by Old Grimsby Sound (see page 48) and enter on a W heading. The area is shallow and dries at LWS. Alternative anchorage is in 2.5m sand, 300m to NE of the quay. The amount of shelter depends on the height of tide and actual position. A cable runs across Green Porth where anchoring is prohibited. The harbour is now only used by a few fishing boats and dayboats on drying moorings. Landing can be made on the sandy beach. Strong tidal streams. The long, narrow dinghy slip to N of Raven's Porth is the private property of the Island Hotel.

Gimble Porth (Tresco)

49°57'.80N 06°20'.30W

Sheltered NE-E-SE-S-SW-W. A rather exposed anchorage in a wide bay approached by Old Grimsby Sound (see page 48). Enter on a S course towards the centre of the bay. Anchor in 2m sand just inside the line joining the two arms of the bay. A drying anchorage is available further inshore but keep a sharp lookout for rocks and stones. Usually deserted.

Rushy Porth at LW

Green Porth, Old Grimsby, at LW

Gimble Porth with Norwethel (left)

Great Popplestone, Bryher, at LW

Great Porth, Bryher (Castle Bryher in distance)

Stoney Porth, Bryher, at LW

Rushy Bay, Bryher

Castle Porth (Tresco)

49°57'.65N 06°20'.90W

Sheltered N-NE-E-SE-S-SW-W. A small anchorage tucked away to the S of Cromwell's Castle, suitable for smaller vessels but affected by swell. Many visitors ashore at the castle.

Great Popplestones (Bryher)

49°57'.20N 06°21'.65W

Sheltered NE-E-SE-S-SW. A dangerous but fascinating anchorage, for use only in very settled conditions by experienced yachtsmen. There is a stony bar across the entrance which is very narrow. Approach on a SE course and enter on an ESE heading to anchor in 1.5m on sand and stones. Most of the anchorage dries at LWS. Beach of sand and rock.

Stinking and Great Porths (Bryher)

49°56'.90N 06°21'.60W

Two anchorages for use in very settled weather; both coves dry at their heads but Great Porth has 1.5m sand some 200m from the head of the cove. Approach keeping Scilly Rock on a stern bearing of 320° and enter either cove on an ENE course with great care. A wide sandy beach with rocks, very close to the Hell Bay Hotel where there is an excellent restaurant and bar. Both anchorages are dangerous in onshore winds or swell.

Stony Porth and South Stony Porth (Bryher)

49°56'.68N 06°21'.50W

These two anchorages are not recommended to visitors. They require considerable care in the approach and entrance because of numerous rocks and, like others described above, can only be used in settled weather. Local knowledge is essential.

Rushy Bay (Bryher)

49°56'.55N 06°21'.10W

Sheltered W-NW-N-NE-E-SE-S. An anchorage in 2m on sand off a beautiful beach but rather exposed and for use only in settled weather. Approach carefully with Works Point at the S end of Bryher on 050° because of isolated rocks. Anchor 200m to S of Works Point. There are other anchorages nearby.

Green Bay (Bryher)

49°57'.00N 06°21'.00W

This anchorage is not suitable for fin-keel yachts unless they are equipped with legs as the anchorage always dries. For vessels which can take the ground Green Bay offers valuable shelter from all except SE winds. Green Bay may be approached with sufficient rise of tide by using Merrick Island as a stern bearing on 080°.

Green Bay, Bryher at LW looking SE towards St Mary's

Bennett Boatyard, Bryher

Bennett Boatyard at the S end of the bay offers facilities including boat storage, emergency repairs, showers and WC by arrangement.

Bar Point (Samson)

49°56'.32N 06°21'.00W

Sheltered N-NE-E-SE-S-SW. Anchor in 2m sand 200m to N of Bar Point but very exposed and only for use in settled weather. Approach with care Works Point (Bryher) on 050° and when Outer Colvel Rocks (Bryher) are abeam approach on a SE heading, leaving Bollard Point 200m to starboard.

West Porth (Samson)

49°56'.00N 06°21'.40W

Sheltered N-NE-E-SE-S. Another anchorage for use only in very settled weather with an approach which needs considerable care.

Approach as for Bar Point (above) with Works Point, Bryher 050°. When the saddle of Samson is due E approach, leaving White Island 100m to starboard but taking great care of the drying rocks which lie less than 200m NNE of White Island. Anchor in 1.5m , 300m offshore on sand and rock. There is often a heavy swell from W – SW.

East Porth (Samson)

49°55'.95N 06°21'.00W

Sheltered S-SW-W-NW. A drying anchorage approached on a NW heading, leaving Green Island off Samson 100m to starboard. Sand and rock. Sandy beach. Only suitable for shallow craft in very settled weather. There are many rocks in the approach and at HW this anchorage is exposed to swell from S.

Yachts at anchor off Bar Point, Samson with Puffin Island and Bryher and Tresco in the background
Mike Lewin-Harris

Samson with Bryher (left) and Tresco (right) in the background
Patrick Roach

Island Hotel and Norwethel looking NNW from Block House Point

FACILITIES

Moorings
24 at New Grimsby, 7 at Old Grimsby, Tresco. £15 per night to 40'. Larger vessels £25 per night. Pay for two nights and third night is free.

Landing Places
On the beaches at New Grimsby and Old Grimsby, avoiding quays, steps and, at Old Grimsby, the long causeway which is the private property of the Island Hotel. On Bryher anywhere in Green Bay or on the beach below The Town but keep clear of the quay and jetty.

Harbourmaster
Tresco: Mr Henry Birch, ☎01720 422792, *Mobile* 07778 601237; also contactable through the estate office on S side of the bay at New Grimsby www.tresco.co.uk

Water
Tap on the quay at the root of the quay at New Grimsby harbour, Tresco for water collection in containers.

Showers & WCs
On Tresco at the New Inn, above New Grimsby with use of the swimming pool included in the price. Open 1000–1800. Public toilets on the quay, New Grimsby and at the estate offices. Public toilets near the church on Bryher. Showers by arrangement with Bennett Boatyard, Bryher ☎07979 393206.

Fuel
By arrangement may be collected in cans from the Tresco estate office.

Chandlery
Limited availability from Bennett Boatyard, Green Bay, Bryher ☎07979 393206 www.bennettboatyard.com and Bryher Boatyard ☎01720 422702 richarddrew@hotmail.co.uk

Engineer
Bryher Marine Engineering ☎01720 423047.

Anneka's Quay, Bryher looking E to New Grimsby, Tresco

Welding and metal fabrication
Ted Langdon, Bryher ☎01720 423136.

Internet
Wi-Fi at the New Inn, Tresco and Fraggle Rock Café, Bryher.

Telephones
Call box by village hall at the top of the hill between New and Old Grimsby. Pay 'phone at the New Inn, Tresco. Call box in The Town on Bryher.

Refuse
On Tresco there are recycling bins on the quay at New Grimsby and at the root of the quay in Old Grimsby. Facilities for refuse disposal are limited on Bryher and non-existent on Samson.

Post Office
Quay Shop, New Grimsby, Tresco (☎01720 424113) 0930–1500 Monday to Friday except Wednesdays 0930–1230. (Faxes may be sent and received) and at Bryher Stores, Norrard (☎01720 422010).

Banks
None, but cheques may be cashed at the Tresco estate office with a bank guarantee card.

Shopping
Tresco Stores, New Grimsby, 0930–1730 Monday to Saturday and closed on Sundays. Fish, meat (fresh and frozen), vegetables, ice, newspapers, wine & spirits. Credit cards accepted. Bryer Stores, Norrard (☎01720 422010) is a well stocked grocery and off-licence. Specialises in home-baked bread, pasties and pies.

Laundry
At the Tresco estate office. Open Monday to Friday 0900–1700 (Closed for lunch 1230–1330). Next day service if delivered by 1200.

Eating out
Island Hotel (☎01720 422883), New Inn (☎01720 422844), Abbey Gardens Café and Quay Shop Tearooms on Tresco. Vine Farm Café (☎01720 423168) inThe Town, Fraggle Rock Café in Norrard (☎01720 422222) and Hell Bay Hotel (☎01720 422947) www.hellbay.co.uk on Bryher.

Churches
St Nicholas C of E at Dolphin Town, Tresco and above Green Bay, Bryher.

Bicycle hire
At the estate office, Tresco (☎01720 422849).

Ferries
Daily from quays at Old and New Grimsby (Boatman's Association and Bryher Boats ☎01720 422886 www.bryherboats.co.uk), Tresco to St Mary's, often via Bryher or St Martin's. Exact times depend on tides and times are posted a day in advance on notice boards. Inter-island ferries depart from Church Quay, below The Town, Bryher and from Bar jetty at LW.

Communications
Direct helicopter flights to Penzance from Tresco (Heliport ☎01720 422970).

Attractions
Tresco Abbey gardens and Valhalla museum, open daily 1000–1600 (☎01720 424105).

HISTORY AND VISITS ASHORE

Tresco

Cromwell's castle guards the northern entrance to the channel between Tresco and Bryher and is a distinctive landmark on the Tresco shoreline, whether one is arriving from seaward or from the S. The castle was built around 1651, soon after the defeat of a Royalist uprising in the islands, led by Sir John Grenville; it was intended as a demonstration of strength by the Parliamentarian government, as well as a defence against the Dutch. This fortification replaced King Charles's castle on the hill above, which had been constructed in the 1550s but was so poorly sited that its guns were powerless to protect the sound. A satellite fort of the castle, The Old Blockhouse, overlooks Old Grimsby harbour on the other side of the island and is a fine vantage-point from which to survey the approaches to that anchorage.

The northern part of the island, with its tracts of exposed heathland and outcrops of granite, is an untamed landscape, accessible only by rough paths. Nevertheless, there is evidence of ancient cairns, earthworks and settlements. There is also a hidden cave and freshwater pool at Piper's Hole, on the NE coast.

Bicycles are the main form of transport, together with tractors and electric buggies for visitors and their luggage. A road links the villages of Old and New Grimsby and Dolphin Town in between as well as the estate buildings and the Abbey. This southern part of the island is in complete contrast to the north – verdant and low-lying with pastures and cottage gardens, woods, lakes and superb beaches rich in beautiful shells.

Presumably encouraged by the presence of fresh water on Tresco, Benedictine monks founded a priory close to the pools in the tenth century. They dedicated it to St Nicholas, that popular saint who is invoked by seafarers, among many supplicants. However, the community could barely survive the harsh living conditions in the islands and the depredations of foreign marauders (over a hundred pirates were apparently executed on Tresco in 1209). The priory was gradually reduced to a 'poor cell of monks' and, by the sixteenth century, had been abandoned. The archways of the original building can be seen today in the Abbey Gardens.

It is hard to believe that these magnificent gardens and their surroundings were created out of a windswept, treeless expanse, overgrown with bramble and gorse and buffeted by salt spray and blown sand. The transformation was achieved by Augustus Smith who, in 1834, acquired the lease of Scilly and the title of Lord Proprietor. He decided to make his residence on Tresco, above the ruins of the priory, and immediately laid out a garden, sheltered at first by the old walls and then by the trees and windbreaks that he planted. His collection of

Hangman Island from Bryher with Cromwell's Castle and King Charles' Castle on Tresco

Statue of Children – Tresco Abbey Gardens

mainland Britain. There is still a flourishing school at New Grimsby – a nice tribute to his endeavours – while the church of St Nicholas was built in 1882 in his memory.

Augustus was succeeded in 1874 by his nephew, Algernon Dorrien Smith, who continued his uncle's good works, both in the garden where he added the major windbreaks, and in other spheres. Like his predecessor he realized that the mild climate of Scilly (with only a 10°C variation in the mean monthly temperature) could be exploited commercially. He therefore encouraged his tenants to plant shelter belts and, at his own expense, imported thousands of bulbs for them to grow. By the end of the nineteenth century the cut flower trade was flourishing and has made an important contribution to the economy of Scilly ever since.

Over the past 25 years or so the population of Tresco has been swelled by the creation of time share cottages which bring visitors to the island for most of the year. In recent years the new development known as the 'Flying Boat Club' has been constructed at New Grimsby, close to the estate office, with private facilities for tenants including a restaurant, bar and spa.

Bryher

The people of Bryher were known as 'thorns' or 'lopsiders', perhaps because they were always leaning into the wind which sweeps in from the Atlantic. The exposed NW coast offers dramatic scenery at Hell Bay and most of the island is open heathland, wild and lonely, with spectacular views from the height of Watch Hill. There are many prehistoric remains, in the form of chamber tombs on Samson Hill and Gweal Hill, a prominent burial mound on Shipman Head Down, where boulder walls link the cairns and a submerged field system at Green Bay on the E coast. This sheltered side of the island was chosen, not surprisingly, as a place of settlement by more recent inhabitants. The small village called The Town is situated above New Grimsby Sound and has two quays; one of granite by the church can be used only at high water while the newer jetty at the Bar, further N is accessible at all stages of the tide. This was originally constructed of wood in three days, thanks to the BBC TV programme 'Challenge Anneka' but has recently been rebuilt and extended with a concrete structure. Bryher prides itself in operating a year-round, inter-island launch service.

sub-tropical plants became famous in his own lifetime and the 17 acres of gardens remain one of the principal attractions of Tresco (see page 83). Within the garden, at Valhalla, he established a fascinating museum of figureheads and other relics taken from ships wrecked around the coasts of Scilly.

Augustus Smith not only changed the face of Tresco, but he revolutionised the existence of the islanders throughout Scilly, rescuing them from the poverty into which they had fallen through the neglect of previous administrators. He reformed the system of land tenure, tackled the problem of smuggling, promoted the shipbuilding industry, removed rocks from the channel between Tresco and Bryher to make it more navigable, persuaded the farmers to grow better varieties of potatoes and introduced compulsory education 40 years ahead of

Valhalla at Tresco Abbey gardens

The church at All Saints, near the main quay, was dedicated in 1742 and later enlarged. Like the school, which closed in 1972, it originally served both Bryher and the neighbouring island of Samson to the S. The church overlooks Green Bay, a drying anchorage frequented by shoal-draft yachts. At the S tip of the island is Rushy Bay, a pretty beach with safe bathing.

Today the residents of Bryher are mainly engaged in tourism. Holiday accommodation is

varied but limited and, in season, many of the locals move out to their greenhouses and garden sheds to make space for the visitors. As in the rest of Scilly, the tourist trade has replaced the traditional occupations of pilotage, salvage and rescue at which the men of Bryher excelled. One of the most famous – and most profitable – incidents occurred in 1910 when the liner *Minnehaha* grounded on Scilly Rock, W of the island. Gigs from Bryher, including the *Czar*, brought passengers, crew and live cargo of cattle to safety while the rest of the cargo was jettisoned and found its way onto the shores of Bryher. The *Czar* is still owned by the same Bryher families who commissioned her in 1879 and participates in the weekly gig races. Just above the jetty at The Bar is the *Sussex* Gig Shed, used as a shelter and information centre. The gig was built in 1888 with proceeds from the salvage and saving of lives from the wrecked steamer of the same name. The gig was last used in 1955 to rescue the crew from the Panamanian ship *Mando* which was wrecked on Golden Ball Brow and became a total loss.

Samson

Humans were present on the island from prehistoric times, evidenced by burial chambers and hut circles on the hills and , on the shore, by traces of field walls running out to sea. More recent settlers established themselves in the S part, increasing from a single family in 1669 to 34 persons by 1822. Despite the bleak terrain they managed to eke out a living, mainly by fishing, kelp making and pilotage. Their diet consisted of potatoes, fish and limpets.

In the early nineteenth century the inhabitants invested in a sailing yawl, *Fly*, to supplement the piloting and salvage work previously carried out in gigs. However, both *Fly* and her larger successor, the cutter *Defiance*, broke their moorings and were driven onto the rocks and the venture failed. The lack of a safe harbour on Samson is something that present-day yachtsmen might bear in mind.

By the 1850s, the dwindling and increasingly ageing community on Samson had ceased to be viable and was probably near starvation. In 1855 Augustus Smith, as Lord Proprietor of Scilly, ordered the evacuation of the two families and three or four households that made up the entire population of the island and re-housed them elsewhere. Only their ruined cottages and overgrown fields remain. Subsequently Augustus Smith grazed cattle on the island and attempted to keep deer there until they took advantage of a low tide and escaped across the channel to Tresco.

Dropnose Point, Bryher with Castle Bryher and Norrard Rocks

**St Martin's view NW with Higher Town Quay and Par beach
in foreground, Round Island beyond** *Patrick Roach*

St Martin's, St Helen's, Tean and Eastern Isles

OVERVIEW

St Martin's

Some two miles long but no more than half a mile across, St Martin's is a long narrow island with a central ridge of granite. At low tide St Martin's is attached to White Island which lies to the N and together they form a land mass of 237 hectares. It has a population of about 110, concentrated largely in the rather grandly named Higher, Middle and Lower Towns. For some unknown reason the people of St Martin's are known as Gannicks! For yachtsmen the most conspicuous feature of the island is the day mark (56m) on St Martin's Head at the E extremity. This 7m high hollow tower was constructed in 1683 (not 1637 as inscribed) and was originally painted white. This caused confusion with St Agnes lighthouse and led to at least one shipwreck in the vicinity. In 1891 its livery was changed to the alternate red and white bands of today. Higher Town Quay has recently been extended and largely rebuilt and there is a second quay at Lower Town, useable at LW.

St Helen's

St Helen's is uninhabited, has an area of 20 hectares and is a smooth, rounded hill (42m) covered in grass and heather.

Tean

This little island of 16 hectares is also uninhabited, mostly barren and deserted except for seabirds, notably ringed plover and tern. During their breeding season from April to July there is a voluntary restriction on landing on Tean.

Eastern Isles

The Eastern Isles are a group of eleven uninhabited islands and numerous rocks that are situated to the SE and S of St Martin's. The largest island, Great Ganilly, has an area of 13 hectares and is 800m long, its highest point being 32m. The islands are deserted but they form an interesting cruising area in settled weather for skilled navigators. The area is shallow and there are numerous isolated rocks but entry and anchorage by fin-keel vessels is possible. The highest point on Great Ganilly (32m) is at the NW end with a saddle and a lower hill (28m) at the SE end and these are important landmarks which can be seen from

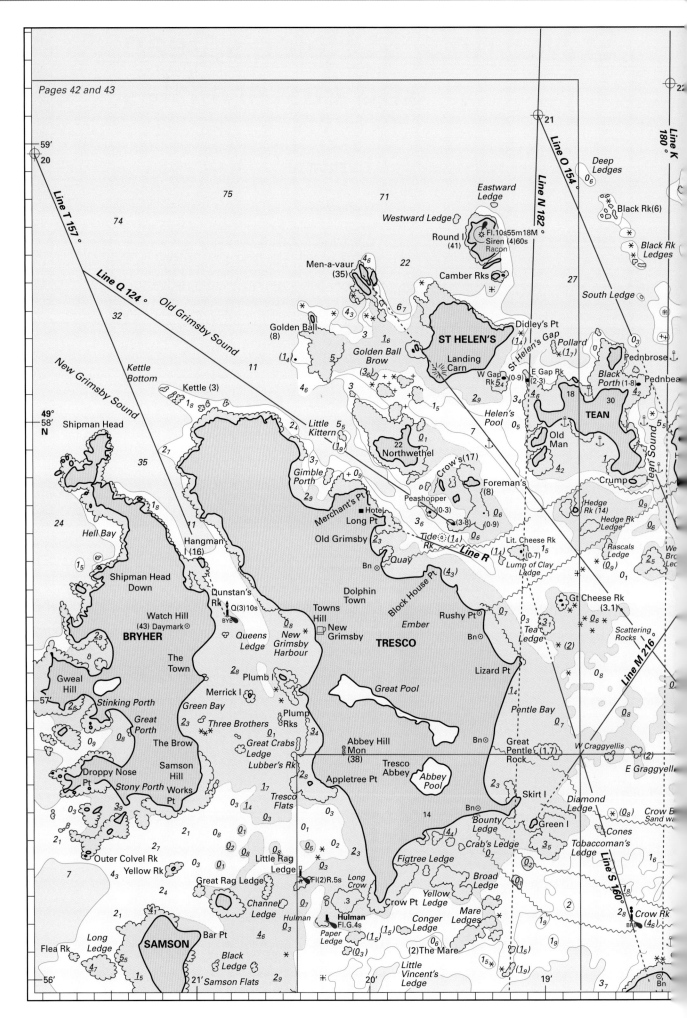

Pages 42 and 43

Line T 157°

Line Q 124°

Old Grimsby Sound

New Grimsby Sound

Line O 154°

Line N 182°

Line K 180°

59'
20

75

74

71

Eastward Ledge

Deep Ledges 0.6

Black Rk(6)

Westward Ledge

Black Rk Ledges

Fl.10s55m18M
Siren (4)60s
Racon

Round I (41)

32

11

Men-a-vaur (35)

22

Camber Rks

27

South Ledge 0.3

6.7

Golden Ball (8)

4.6

Didley's Pt

ST HELEN'S

(1.4)

Pollard

Pednbrose

3

Golden Ball Brow

1.6

(1.7)

Pednbea

Kettle Bottom

Kettle (3)

(1.4)

1.8

5

(3.6)

Landing Carn

St Helen's Gap

W Gap Rk 5.4

E Gap Rk (2.3)

4.6

18

Black Porth (1.8)

30

TEAN

4.2

4.6

4.6

3

Helen's Pool 0.5

2.9

3.4

49°
58'
N

Shipman Head

35

2.7

2.4

Little Kittern 5.5

(1.9)

22

Northwethel 0.1

7

Old Man

1

5.5

18

1.8

Hell Bay

1.5

24

Gimble Porth

3.7

+ 0.9

2.9

Crow's(17)

Foreman's (8)

4.2

Crump

Hedge Rk (14)

Hedge Rk Ledge 0.6

Merchant's Pt

Hotel

Long Pt

Peashopper

(0.3)

3.6

(3.8)

0.6

(0.9)

Rascals Ledge (0.9)

0.1

2.5

Hangman I (16)

Old Grimsby

2.3

Rk

Tide Rk (1.4)

0.6

Lit. Cheese Rk

(1.4)

(0.7)

1.5

Lump of Clay Ledge

Shipman Head Down

11

Dunstan's Rk

Q(3)10s

Quay

Bn

Block House Pt

(4.3)

Line R

Gt Cheese Rk (3.1)

(0.7)

0.6

Scattering Rocks

Watch Hill (43) Daymark

BYB

0.8

Queens Ledge

New Grimsby Harbour

Towns Hill

Dolphin Town

New Grimsby

TRESCO

Rushy Pt

0.7

0.3

3.1

Tea Ledge

0.6

Line M 216°

BRYHER

The Town

2.8

Plumb I

Ember

Bn

(2)

0

2.9

8

Merrick I

Green Bay

2.3

Three Brothers

Plump Rks

3.4

Great Pool

Lizard Pt

1.4

0.8

Gweal Hill

57'

2.6

Stinking Porth

Great Porth

0.8

The Brow

0.9

2.3

Great Crabs Ledge

Lubber's Rk

0.1

Abbey Hill Mon (38)

Pentle Bay

0.7

Bn

Great Pentle Rock

(1.7)

W Craggyellis

(2)

E Graggyell

Droppy Nose Pt

Stony Porth

Samson Hill Works Pt

2.8

1.7

Tresco Flats

0.3

1.4

0.3

0.3

Tresco Abbey

Appletree Pt

14

2.3

Skirt I

Diamond Ledge

(0.8)

Crow B Sand

3.9

0.3

0.3

0.1

Abbey Pool

Bounty Ledge

2.3

Green I

3.5

Cones

Tobaccoman's Ledge

1.6

2.1

2.7

2.1

0.8

0.1

0.2

0.8

0.8

0.5

0.2

0.7

0.2

Crab's Ledge

(4.4)

0.7

0.2

0.8

Outer Colvel Rk

Yellow Rk

0.3

0.1

Little Rag Ledge

0.3

2.3

Figtree Ledge

Yellow Ledge

Broad Ledge

0.1

1.9

(2)

7

4.3

Great Rag Ledge

Fl(2)R.5s

Long Crow

Crow Pt

Mare Ledges

1.8

2.8

Crow Rk (4.6)

2.4

Channel Ledge

0.7

.3

Conger Ledge

0.6

1.9

2.1

4.1

Hulman

Hulman Fl.G.4s

0.3

Paper Ledge

(1.5)

(1.5)

(1.5)

1.5

(1.9)

3.7

Long Ledge

5.5

Bar Pt

4.6

Black Ledge

(0.3)

(2)*The Mare*

0.6

Bn

Flea Rk

4.7

1.5

56'

SAMSON

21' *Samson Flats*

2.9

Little Vincent's Ledge

20'

19'

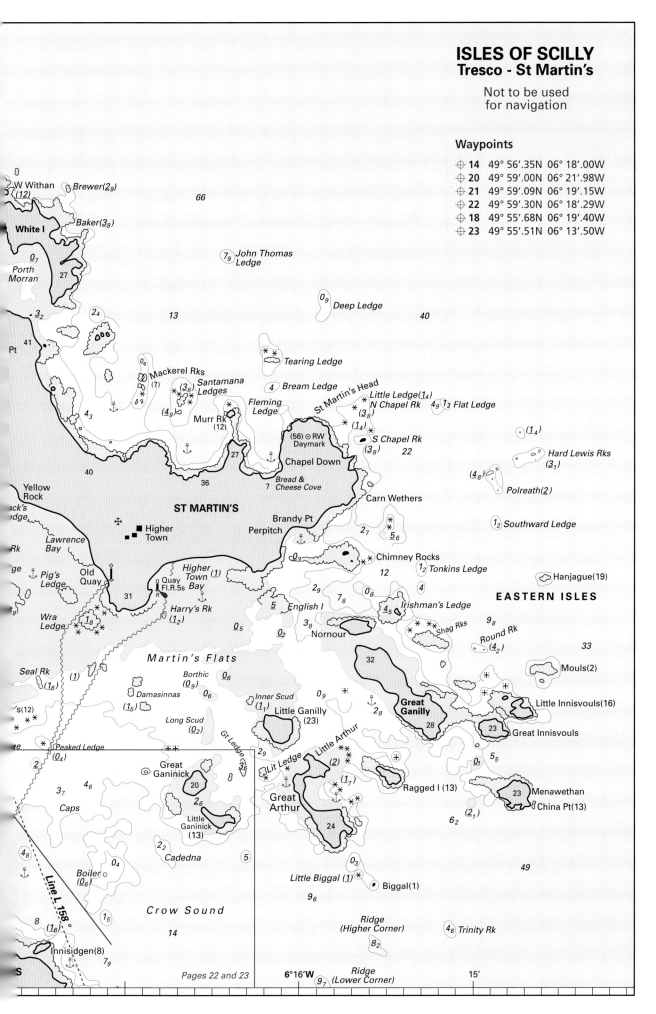

ISLES OF SCILLY
Tresco - St Martin's

Not to be used
for navigation

Waypoints

⊕ **14** 49° 56'.35N 06° 18'.00W
⊕ **20** 49° 59'.00N 06° 21'.98W
⊕ **21** 49° 59'.09N 06° 19'.15W
⊕ **22** 49° 59'.30N 06° 18'.29W
⊕ **18** 49° 55'.68N 06° 19'.40W
⊕ **23** 49° 55'.51N 06° 13'.50W

W Withan
Brewer(2₉)
(12)
Baker(3₈)
White I
0₇
Porth
Morran
27
66
2₄
13
40
3 2
41
Pt
4₃
Mackerel Rks
(7)
Santamana
Ledges
(3₆)
(4₉)
Murr Rk
(12)
Fleming
Ledge
John Thomas
Ledge
7₉
0₉ Deep Ledge
Tearing Ledge
Bream Ledge 4
St Martin's Head
Little Ledge(1₄)
N Chapel Rk
(3₈)
(1₄)
S Chapel Rk
(3₈)
4₉ 1₂ Flat Ledge
(1₄)
Hard Lewis Rks
(3₁)
Polreath(2)
(4₈)
(56) ⊙ RW
Daymark
22
40
36
7
27
Chapel Down
Bread &
Cheese Cove
ST MARTIN'S
Carn Wethers
Yellow
Rock
ack's
edge
Lawrence
Bay
Higher
Town
Brandy Pt
Perpitch
2₇
5₆
Southward Ledge
1₂
Chimney Rocks
Tonkins Ledge
1₂
Hanjague(19)
EASTERN ISLES
Rk
Pig's
Ledge
ge
Old
Quay
31
Quay
Fl.R.5s
R
Higher
Town
Bay
(1)
Harry's Rk
(1₂)
0₃
12
2₉
7₈
5
English I
0₆
3₈
Nornour
0₅
4₅
Irishman's Ledge
4
Shag Rks
9₈
Round Rk
(4₂)
33
Wra
Ledge
1₈
Martin's Flats
Borthic
(0₉)
0₆
0₂
32
Great
Ganilly
28
Mouls(2)
Little Innisvouls(16)
Seal Rk
(1₆)
(1)
Damasinnas
(1₅)
0₆
Inner Scud
(1₁)
Little Ganilly
(23)
0₉
2₈
Great Innisvouls
23
's(12)
Long Scud
(0₂)
Gt Ledge
2₉
Lit Ledge
Little Arthur
(2)
(1₇)
Ragged I (13)
0₁
5₅
23
Menawethan
China Pt(13)
(2₁)
Peaked Ledge
(0₄)
2
Great
Ganinick
3₆
Great
Arthur
24
6₂
49
3₇
4₆
Caps
20
2₆
Little
Ganinick
(13)
2₂
Cadedna
5
4₈
Boiler
(0₆)
0₄
1₅
0₃
Little Biggal (1)
Biggal(1)
9₆
Crow Sound
14
Ridge
(Higher Corner)
8₂
Trinity Rk
4₆
Line L 158°
8
(1₆)
Innisidgen(8)
7₉

Hanjague, Chimney Rocks and Eastern Isles looking E from Perspitch Bay, St Martin's

afar. Hanjague, a steep sided pyramid-shaped rock (19m) is another easily recognised feature. St Martin's daymark (red and white banded tower, 56m) is also an important reference point. In settled weather the Eastern Isles offer several delightful anchorages for experienced yachtsmen but are only recommended for a daytime stop.

PASSAGES

Tean Sound and St Helen's Gap are the two most used passages from the north into the main anchorages to the W of St Martin's although the approach through the latter can only be made when there is sufficient height of tide.

St Helen's Gap

Access to St Helen's Pool from the N is via St Helen's Gap with a minimum depth of 0.5m and a minimum width of 100m.

Tidal Streams

No information is available about the streams running through this channel but they should be similar to those shown on page 45.

Buoys and beacons

Round Island
Lighthouse Fl.10s55m18M Horn(4)60s Racon(M)

Leading marks

Line N
Star Castle Hotel (St Mary's) in line with E Gap Rock (2.3m) on 182° from ⊕21

Entrance to St Helen's Pool from N

East Gap Rock   Merchant's Point   West Gap Rock

Entrances to Tean and St Helen's Sounds looking SW
Patrick Roach

Tean   Tresco   East Gap Rock   West Gap Rock   St Helens   Round Island   Man-a-V

Directions

From a position NNE of Round Island ($\oplus$21) leave the E coast of Round Island about 250m to starboard and steer due S to hold Didley's Point (the easternmost point of St Helen's) about 100m to starboard (line N). St Helen's Gap should then bear approximately SSW between East Gap Rock (2.3m) to port and West Gap Rock (0.9m) to starboard. Approach with care to make good a course of 200° and give nothing to port until East Gap Rock is abeam. If necessary head up to West Gap Rock as shallows and rock extend from East Gap to the NW for 50m or so. Then bear away to the S and take soundings over the shallowest part of the bar between Old Man and St Helen's (charted depth 0.5m). The rock formations constituting the East Gap and the West Gap dry to between 4.6m and 5.5m at low water springs but there is still about 3m depth between them. The sand bar begins about 200m beyond an imaginary line joining the two gap rocks and, beyond the bar, there is enough water to anchor, always afloat, in almost all parts of the Pool. Although the sand bar cannot be crossed at LWS the chart shows there is 2m of water available at St Mary's Pool at Low Water Neaps so it is likely that the St Helen's Gap entrance will more often than not be available – with care - to vessels drawing 1.8m. It would probably not inconvenience anyone if a yacht anchored in calm conditions in St Helen's Gap before entering St Helen's Pool after LWS when entry from the N must await sufficient height of tide.

Tean Sound

The approach from seaward is strewn with rocky islets, rocks and submerged ledges. Eyeball navigation is essential and, given a choice of other northern Scilly anchorages, one might prefer any of them even in calm conditions and good visibility.

Tidal Streams

There is no information about the streams through Tean Sound but they should be similar to those for Old Grimsby Sound given on page 49.

Tean Sound view N with St Martin's (right) and Tean (left) with St Helen's, Men-a-Vaur and Round Island beyond
Patrick Roach

Tidal streams

NE of St Martin's

Local HW	Plymouth HW	Dover HW	Direction	Rate (knots) Spring	Neaps
−0505	−0600	+0045	NNW	1.1	0.5
−0205	−0300	+0345	N	1.6	0.8
+0055	0000	−0540	SE	2.1	1.0
+0355	+0300	−0240	SSW	1.4	0.7
+0555	+0600	+0020	NNW	1.0	0.5

Note: Stream reaches 2.3 knots at HW Plymouth +1H in springs.

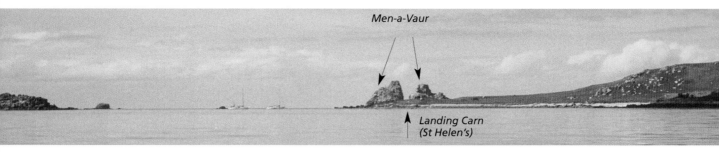

Men-a-Vaur

Landing Carn
(St Helen's)

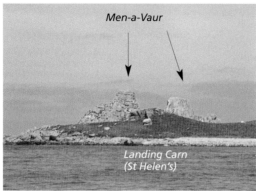

*St Helen's Pool,
looking NW;
centre of Men-a-
Vaur in line with
St Helen's
Landing Carn on
322° (line G)*

Men-a-Vaur

Landing Carn
(St Helen's)

Warning

As will be seen from the table on page 45 tidal streams can be strong in the approach and must be allowed for when entering as they will be abeam.

Buoys and beacons

Round Island
Lighthouse Fl.10s55m18M Horn(4)60s Racon(M)

Leading marks

Leading into Tean Sound

Line K
TV tower just open Goat's Point on 180°20′ leads E of Black Rock (from ⊕22)

Line O
Bab's Carn on Pednbean on 154° leads W of Black Rock (from ⊕21)

Leading out of Tean Sound

Line L
Guther's Island on 158° with Toll's Island open to E and Innisidgen open W

Crosses the shallow flats

Line M
Green Island (Tresco) on 216°

Leads to Hats buoy

Line G
Centre of Men-a-Vaur in line with St Helen's Landing Carn on 322° leads NW/SE to and from Dt Helen's Pool

Leads to Crow Rock beacon

Line S
Crow Rock beacon on TV Tower (160°30′) towards St Mary's Road (see photos page 49)

Directions

It is best to approach Tean Sound just after low water when the hazards are most visible. There are two lines of transit (see photos page 63) of which the north western transit (Line O, which will be described first) is the preferred route. From a position 0.4M NNE of Round Island (⊕21) steer 154° for Pednbean rock (1.8m) in line with Bab's Carn (20m) on the W end of St Martin's, taking care, in this approach, of the string of rocks just 200m to port; Deep Ledges (0.6m), Black Rock (6m) and associated rocks, Black Rock Ledges and South Ledge (drying 1.4m). When abeam of Pednbrose (12m) to starboard do not stray to port if the tide is low as Corner Rock has a charted depth of only 0.3m. Almost immediately afterwards, however, bear away to port in a southeasterly direction until the channel opens to the S and then steer S on the western tip of visible land on St Martin's. Give nothing to starboard to avoid Thongyore Ledge which lies about 200m NW of Goat's Point. You may however need to borrow to starboard 100m NW of Goat's Point in order to keep the deeper water of the main channel. This course should bring a yacht into the narrow sound between Tean and St Martin's.

The northern transit (Line K) offers the first possible entry into a northern Scilly harbour when arriving from the E. Observation of Round Island light approximately to the SW and St Martin's daymark approximately to the SE should assist in gaining a position due N of the entrance to Tean Sound (⊕22). From here the TV tower on St Mary's just open of Goat's Point at the W tip of St Martin's bears 180°. On the approach alter course to SW when Lion (8m) bears SE to clear off-lying rocks and alter course after 150m to SE to pick up the transit again. When Plumb Island is abeam to port, borrow 100m to the E for 100m to clear Rough Ledge. Off Tinkler's Point follow the directions in the previous transit (see above) to steer S on the westernmost point of St Martin's.

Lines L and M lead S out of Tean Sound and across the shallow flats towards St Mary's Road when there is sufficient height of tide.

MAIN ANCHORAGES AND MOORINGS

St Helen's Pool (St Helen's)

Sheltered N-NE-E-SE-S-SW-W-NW. Although it is only about a half mile dinghy trip to Old Grimsby Harbour (depending on the state of the tide) this anchorage offers seclusion, fine views and good holding in 2m to 7m sand for those prepared to put up with a complete lack of nearby facilities. The roadstead was once used by quite large vessels and, although one cannot describe the pool as landlocked, the islands, rocks and banks around it do in fact create this effect except at high water when, in the prevailing westerlies, the Atlantic breaks across the rocks of Golden Ball Brow to the NW. Even then these extensive rocks afford some shelter from the outside swell and the tide flows more slowly in most parts of the pool than in other more restricted Scillonian anchorages. If, while in St Helen's Pool, the wind blows up from any direction, one can move to other more protected parts of the pool in the lee of land or rocks. The anchorage is sheltered from all directions at low water but strong winds from the NW, NE and SE may produce uncomfortable conditions and some swell, especially around high water. Yachtsmen may wish to take anchor bearings, in which case the Church tower at Dolphin Town on Tresco to the SW, the leading carn on the W end of St Helen's and the conspicuous Hedge Rock to the SE are useful in most parts of the pool. In places Round Island light can be seen to the N behind St Helen's Island.

Tean Sound (St Martin's)

Sheltered NE-E-SE-S-SW-W-NW. Subject to swell. This sound forms the seaway between Tean and St Martin's and, at its narrowest point, the gap between the low water rocks is only about 100m. Charted depths in the sound between Thongyore Ledge and Southward Carn (the SW point of St Martin's) are, from N to S, 5.5m, 8.2m, 8.2m and 7.3m so it is quite deep and the bottom is mostly rock. In the deep water the St Martin's on the Isle Hotel (☎01720 422092) has installed six moorings for the use of visiting yachts. Visitors who utilise the hotel's restaurant do not have to pay for an overnight mooring but a charge of £10 is made for use of the showers and swimming pool. Yachtsmen determined to anchor should ensure their ground tackle can cope with the rock bottom, the spring flow of 2 knots or more and the need

Yachts at anchor in St Helen's Pool
Patrick Roach

orwethel   Men-a-Vaur   St Helens   Round Island

Lower Town Quay, St Martin's with Tean and Round Island
Mike Lewin-Harris

for a lot of scope on their anchor chain. Swell can also be a problem. Alternatively anchor just SW of Crump Island out of the main tidal stream. Lower Town Quay is unlit but has a beacon with a ⟨ topmark. Don't obstruct the quay or leave your dinghy on it; use the beach. It is a short walk uphill to the Seven Stones Pub (☎ 01720 423560) where food is served.

MINOR ANCHORAGES

Higher Town Bay (St Martin's)

49°57'.45N 06°16'.65W
Sheltered W-NW-N-NE. An open bay anchorage with a sandy bottom that dries and is easy to approach. There is a fine sandy beach

(see photo page 58). Higher Town, with its shop and post office, lies on the hill above the anchorage. Some isolated rocks. Higher Town Quay at the W end of the bay has been largely rebuilt and extended recently and has a red beacon (Fl.R.5s) and ■ topmark. There are public WCs close to the quay.

Perpitch (St Martin's)

49°57'.55N 06°16'.00W
Sheltered W-NW. A small anchorage which needs care on entering because of off-lying rocky shoals. Approach on a SW course and anchor in 1.5m sand. Small sandy beach which is normally deserted.

Perspitch Bay, St Martin's

Stony Porth/Bread and Cheese Cove (St Martin's)

49°57'.85N 06°16'.20W

Sheltered E-SE-S-SW-W. A beautiful anchorage beneath the day mark with rocky sides and an approach which needs care. Approach on a SW or SE course to avoid Tearing Ledge. Anchor in 5m sand and rock. Normally deserted.

Bull's Porth (St Martin's)

49°57'.85N 06°16'.50W

Sheltered E-SE-S-SW-W. An anchorage with rocky sides which needs care on the approach. This should be on a SSW heading leaving Murr Rock 100m to port and keeping well clear. Anchor in 5m sand. The cove is usually deserted.

St Martin's Bay (Great Bay and Little Bay) (St Martin's)

49°58'.00N 06°17'.15W

Sheltered E-SE-S-SW-W-NW. A wide bay with several anchorages which need great care in the approach between the many rocky ledges. Approach on a S course leaving Great Merrick Ledge 150m to starboard and then Mackerel Rocks 150m to port, taking great care to leave Little Ledge of Mackerel Rocks to starboard. Anchor in 3m sand. Large sandy beach which usually has some visitors.

Porth Morran (St Martin's)

49°58'.50N 06°17'.55W

Sheltered NE-E-SE-S-SW-W. An anchorage between St Martin's and White Island, with some protection from W behind rocks and islands, which offers best shelter at LW. The approach requires care and should be made on a S heading, leaving White Island 200m to port. Anchor in 3m on sand and rock. White Island is often visited by tourists. Stony beach and shallow caves.

Bread and Cheese Cove, St Martin's

Bull's Porth, St Martin's

St Martin's Bay looking NW to White Island

Porth Morran, looking NW with White Island (R)

Lawrence's Bay (St Martin's)

49°57'.60N 06°17'.40W

A wide, flat bay and drying anchorage really only suitable for very shallow draft craft with local knowledge, owing to the large number of rocky shoals in the approach.

Warning

If approaching anchorages in the Eastern Isles from the S or E great care should be taken to avoid Renny Rock, an awash rock 200m W of Menawethan and effectively in the channel between that island and Ragged Island.

East Porth (Great Ganilly, Eastern Isles)

49°57'.10N 06°15'.20W

Sheltered S-SW-W-NW. An anchorage in 1 to 2m sand and stones that has an approach with many isolated rocks. Hanjague, a distinctive steep, pyramid shaped rock, on a stern bearing of 054° leads through, but very close to, the rocks. Deserted.

West Porth (Great Ganilly, Eastern Isles)

49°57'.00N 06°15'.50W

Sheltered SW-W-NW-N-NE-E. An anchorage in 1 to 2m sand, well protected but exposed at HW to W. From Crow Sound Anchorage, and on a course of 080°, locate Biggal rock(1m). This rock is 300m to SSE of Great Arthur; leave it to port and continue on this course. Finally, when 100m from Great Ganilly, follow the coast at 100m on a NW course and thence to West Porth. There is a safe deep-water anchorage (5m sand) 300m to N of Ragged Island but this is more exposed to NW winds. Deserted.

Arthur Porth (Great Arthur, Eastern Isles)

49°56'.67N 06°15'.75W

Sheltered SW-W-NW-N. An anchorage in 1.5m sand lying between Great and Little Arthur with several rocks near its entrance which require care. Approach Ragged Island on a N course and when 50m from it turn to a W heading and enter the anchorage with care. Deserted.

Middle Arthur (Eastern Isles)

49°56'.70N 06°16'.10W

Sheltered SW-W-NW-N-NE-E. A day anchorage in calm weather in 2m sand and weed off Arthur Quay. Approach with care on a N course from between Little Ganinick and Great Arthur. Deserted.

FACILITIES

Moorings

6 in Tean Sound; contact St Martin's on the Isle Hotel, ☎ 01720 422092 or through local boat *Voyager*.

Landing Places

3 quays – at Lower Town, near St Martin's on the Isle Hotel; at Higher Town, E of Cruther's Hill (dries at LW) and at Old Quay, W of Cruther's Hill (dries at half tide). Ideally avoid all these and leave tenders on adjacent beaches.

Water

In containers by arrangement with the hotel (see moorings above).

Refuse

Rubbish at hotel (separated into glass, cans and burnable items).

Showers & WCs

By arrangement with the hotel – swimming pool use included. Public WCs at New Quay.

Telephones

Call boxes in Middle and Higher Towns. Payphone at the hotel.

Post Office

At St Martin's general stores, Higher Town (☎ 01720 422801 or 422893).

Shopping

General stores, Higher Town. Frozen food, off licence, newspapers to order. Open 0900–1230 and 1330-1730 Monday to Saturday and 1000–1100 Sunday. Lindy's Locker in Lower Town for fruit and vegetables. Bakery, Coffee shop and takeaway pizzas at Higher Town in season (☎ 01720 423444).

Eating out

St Martin's on the Isle Hotel (☎ 01720 422092). Little Arthur Café, Higher Town (☎ 01720 422457). Seven Stones Pub (☎ 01720 423560). Polreath Guest House and tearoon, Higher Town (☎ 01720 422046 www.polreath.com)

Church

C of E near Higher Town.

Ferries

Regular service from Lower Town and Higher Town quays to St Mary's and other islands.

Divers

Diving school and services ☎ 01720 422848

HISTORY AND VISITS ASHORE

St Martin's

The headland and nearby Chapel Down at the eastern extremity of St Martin's offer splendid views across Scilly and, in particular, the Eastern Isles to the S and the Seven Stones reef to the NE. A lightship has been maintained near the reef since 1842 but, unfortunately, did not prevent the infamous disaster which occurred when the tanker *Torrey Canyon* which steamed onto the reef in 1967 while trying to take a short cut around Land's End. In clear conditions it is possible to see the mainland too. One can easily imagine how, in a far distant age before sea levels rose, the land did not end at Land's End but extended to Scilly via the Seven Stones. There is ample evidence that the sea has continued to encroach in relatively recent times. For instance, at Par Beach in Higher Town Bay on the S side of the island, submerged fields are shown by the remains of stone walls visible below the high tide line.

As the easternmost point of Scilly, St Martin's seems to have been the landfall for the earliest settlers. The first arrived from Cornwall in about 2000 BC and lived largely on a diet of limpets, according to excavations on English Island (now more shoal than island), off the SE coast. They left numerous burial chambers and field systems throughout St Martin's as well as the oldest known statue in Britain which now stands as a cairn on Chapel Down. House foundations and pieces of pottery have also been discovered at Par Beach dating from the later Romano-British period although the most important find was at Nornour, SE of English Island. The sixteenth century saw a further influx to St Martin's from Sennen in Cornwall and gave the inhabitants their supposed characteristics of red or sandy hair and blue eyes.

The island can be explored on foot in a convenient circuit which highlights the contrast between the rugged N coast with its spectacular rock-strewn bays with beautiful sandy beaches and the gentler S side, sloping down to shallow waters of an incredible blue. Above the beaches, fields have been hedged-in to take advantage of the light, sandy soil and these sun-traps produce the earliest flowers in Scilly. St Martin's vineyard, just inland from Par beach, is the most southerly in the UK and is open for conducted tours, the sale of wine and home grown lavender (☎ 01720 423418 www.stmartinsvinyard.co.uk). In addition to bulb growing, the islanders catch fish, especially lobster and crab. However, tourism has become the chief occupation and there are now numerous holiday homes, a hotel and campsite to accommodate visitors. In the eighteenth century the kelp industry flourished. Kelp, an ingredient in the manufacture of iodine, soap and glass, was produced by burning seaweed in special pits, examples of which survive on White Island.

Stone cairns
St Martin's

St Helen's

On the S shore the ruins of a chapel mark the earliest recorded Christian building in Scilly. St Elidius lived here as a hermit in the tenth century and gave his name, in corrupted form, to the island. A service is held at the site on the Sunday closest to the saints feast day on 8th August. Nearby are the remains of a pest house built in the mid-eighteenth century, used to quarantine disease-ridden seamen arriving from abroad. In those days, before the advent of steamships, the Isles were a major port of call for sailing vessels and St Helen's Pool itself was an alternative anchorage to St Mary's. From the top of St Helen's one can look across to the distinctive jagged peaks of Men-a Vaur and to the lighthouse on Round Island. This white tower (55m) was constructed in 1887 at the expense of the resident colony of puffins which was frightened off when the workmen began collecting their eggs for food.

Tean

Much of the seaweed for the Kelp was gathered on Tean where families from St Martin's would move for the summer. The ruins of their cottages can still be seen. This little island of 16 hectares has also been used for grazing cattle in the past.

Eastern Isles

The Eastern Isles, sheltered from the W, benefit from more soil and grass than many of the deserted islands. Their attractive scenery, wild flowers, seabirds and seals make them a popular destination for day trippers brought by local boatmen and their launches. The island of Nornour which can be reached by crossing the rocky bar from Great Ganilly at LW is of particular interest. It is the site of an ancient village where a remarkable collection of Roman jewellery and other artefacts were discovered. Many of these finds can be seen in the St Mary's museum.

St Agnes from W with Burnt Island in foreground and Gugh in the background
Patrick Roach

St Agnes, Gugh, Annet and the Western Rocks

OVERVIEW

St Agnes and Gugh

The two small islands of St Agnes and Gugh (pronounced like 'new') together measure roughly one mile each way and make up an area of 148 hectares. They are linked by a sand bar – The Bar – which usually covers at HW. St Agnes has a permanent population of about 70 people, mostly engaged in flower growing and tourism but Gugh is uninhabited except for two holiday homes near the beach.

Annet and the Western Rocks

Annet is the largest island W of St Agnes with an area of 21 hectares. It consists of low hills linked by a saddle and has a conspicuous line of tooth-like rocks off its N tip. From Annet to the Western Rocks, a horseshoe-shaped chain of islets and rocks extends over two miles while further outcrops, including Bishop Rock, are scattered to the extreme W and NW. These isolated rocks and ledges, many of them partly submerged, their associated overfalls and currents and the force of the Atlantic swell combine to make the waters of W Scilly especially dangerous.

PASSAGES

The Cove has one of the simplest approaches from the E and also from the S providing that careful attention is paid to the cautionary advice on page 16 about giving the Bishop Rock light and the Pol Bank a wide berth. Access to the northern anchorages of St Agnes and Gugh from St Mary's Sound, Smith Sound, Broad Sound and the North West Passage should not be undertaken except in calm conditions with good visibility.

The Cove

For the distant approach see directions for St Mary's Sound on page 24. About a mile off the S coast of St Agnes the bay known as The Cove will open up to starboard. A yacht may enter when the prominent rock called The Cow is sighted in the middle of the bar, bearing approximately NNW. Keep The Cow in the middle of the bar and proceed straight in to find the anchorage toward the head of the cove.

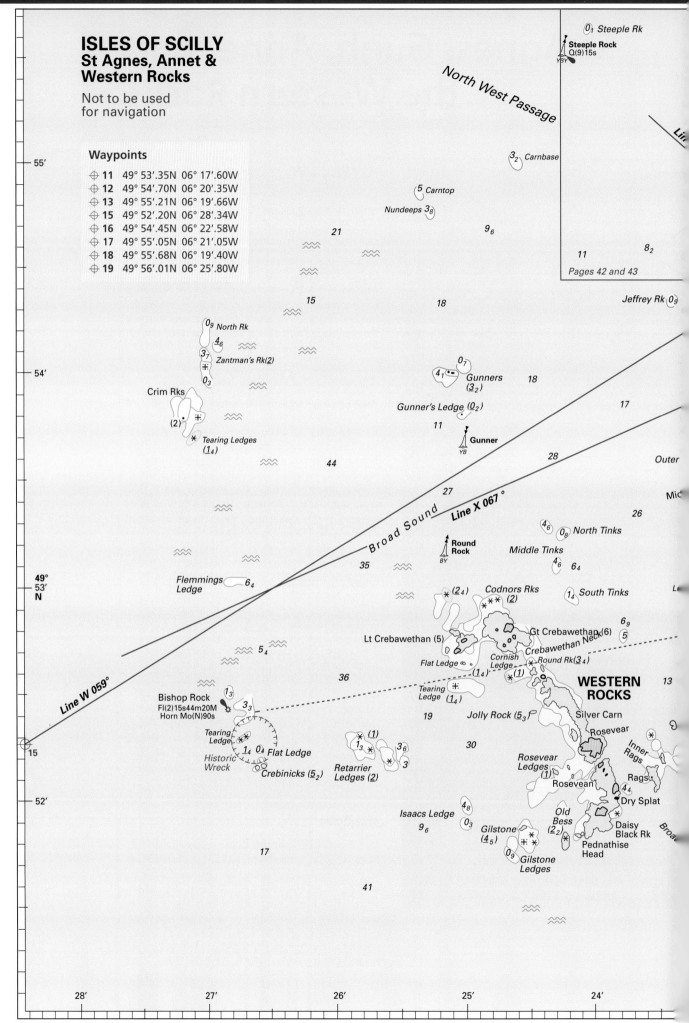

ISLES OF SCILLY
St Agnes, Annet &
Western Rocks

Not to be used
for navigation

Waypoints
⊕ 11   49° 53'.35N 06° 17'.60W
⊕ 12   49° 54'.70N 06° 20'.35W
⊕ 13   49° 55'.21N 06° 19'.66W
⊕ 15   49° 52'.20N 06° 28'.34W
⊕ 16   49° 54'.45N 06° 22'.58W
⊕ 17   49° 55'.05N 06° 21'.05W
⊕ 18   49° 55'.68N 06° 19'.40W
⊕ 19   49° 56'.01N 06° 25'.80W

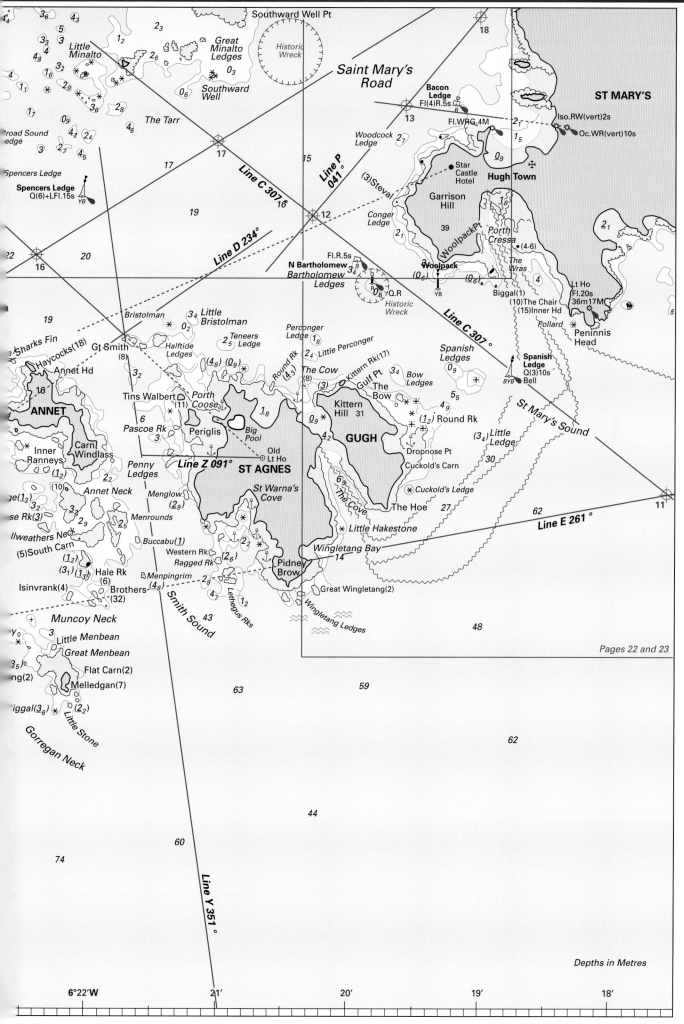

Depths in Metres

Smith Sound

This deep sound separates Annet from St Agnes and offers an alternative route to that of St Mary's Sound for vessels approaching from the S. The approach to the sound requires some care due to many unmarked dangers on either side of the entrance but there are good leading marks for use in fair visibility. The sound is un-buoyed and there is a mediocre anchorage off Annet. Minimum depth 2.5m, minimum width 200m.

Leading marks

Line Y

Castle Bryher between the summits of Great Smith on 351° leads up Smith Sound

Line Z

Old lighthouse on St Agnes on Penny Ledges on 091°

Line D

Carn Irish (Annet) open N of Great Smith clears Halftide Ledges and Bristolman Rock on 234° (stern transit)

Warning

The tidal streams from North West Passage, St Mary's Sound and Smith Sound interact about 600m to N of Great Smith and should be allowed for by taking frequent navigational fixes.

Directions

Approach the old lighthouse on St Agnes on a N course and, when about 1½M from the island, Great Smith will be seen through the sound. Bring this rock onto 351° and, with Castle Bryher between its' summits (Line Y), enter the sound. When the S point of St Agnes is abeam borrow to the E bringing Castle Bryher just E of Great Smith in order to give a good berth to Menpingrim (dries 4.8m), Buccabu (dries1.0m) and an un-named rock (awash) 80m to SE of Buccabu. Half way through the sound when the old lighthouse is abeam and in line with Penny Ledges (line Z) borrow to the W of line Y and bring Castle Bryher just clear of W of Great Smith so as to avoid Pascoe Rock (covers 3m), a shoal (covers 2.5m) and The Quoins (covers 3.2m). Leave Great Smith 200m to starboard and round it onto a NE course towards St Mary's Road. Keep N of line O, Carn Irish open N of Great Smith 234° (stern transit) to clear Bristolman (awash).

Broad Sound

The approach from the SW is via a long straight sound which is buoyed and commences close to the easily recognised Bishop Rock lighthouse. However, the leading marks are distant and good visibility is required. There are no suitable anchorages until St Mary's Road or, ideally, St Mary's Pool are reached. Tidal streams are strong in the SW part of this sound as far as Old Wreck buoy and they sometimes set across the line of approach. Minimum depth 13.9m, minimum width 600m.

Buoys

Round Rock

N cardinal buoy, black over yellow ⬍ topmark, established about 300m N of Round Rock (dries 2.4m)

Gunner

S cardinal pillar buoy, yellow over black, ⬍ topmark, marks Gunners Ledge, awash 300m to N of buoy

Old Wreck

N cardinal pillar buoy (VQ), black over yellow, ⬍ topmark, marks Old Wreck Rock (covers 1m) 150m to S of buoy

Leading marks

Line W

N summit of Great Ganilly just open N of Bant's Carn on 059° leads into St Mary's Road from ⊕15

Line X

Star Castle Hotel in line with the N of Haycocks leads into Broad Sound entrance on 067°. Do not mistake Ruddy (dries 4.3m and lies 200m to WNW of Haycocks) for the N of Haycocks itself

Warning

During spring tides there are heavy overfalls on either side of Broad Sound over and near the rocky shoals in the neighbourhood of Bishop Rock, Flemming's Ledge and Crim Rocks. The stream sometimes sets across the leading line until Old Wreck buoy is passed. An historic wreck is located SE of the Bishop Rock and anchoring, fishing and diving there are prohibited (see plans pages 18 and 72).

Tidal streams

At the N end of Smith Sound stream begins:

Local HW	Devonport HW	Dover HW	Direction	Max rate (knots) Springs	Neaps	Remarks
−0235	−0330	+0330	S	2	–	Generally in
+0225	+0130	−0355	N	2	–	direction of the sound

Tidal streams

In Broad Sound:

Local HW	Plymouth HW	Dover HW	Direction	Rate (knots)	
				Spring	Neaps
−0505	−0600	+0045	NW	0.4	0.2
−0205	−0300	+0345	E	1.0	0.4
+0055	0000	−0540	SE	0.2	0.1
+0355	+0300	−0240	SW	1.2	0.5
+0555	+0600	+0020	NW	1.2	0.5

Directions

Approach the Bishop Rock lighthouse on an E course and, when ¾ M short of it, identify line W or, in poor visibility, line X. Then approach on 059° if using Line W from ⊕15 or 067° if using Line X. On both of these courses leave Flemming's Ledge to port. From here a course of 059°, using Line W, leaves Round Rock buoy to starboard, Gunner buoy 200m to port and Old Wreck buoy close to starboard, continuing into St Mary's Road. When approaching Old Wreck buoy do not stray to port: Jeffrey Rock with a charted depth of 0.9m lies about 800m approximately W of the buoy and about 400m from Line W.

St Mary's Road

If approaching St Agnes or Gugh from St Mary's Pool the safest option is to keep well to the W of the shoals at North Bartholomew, Perconger Ledge and Little Perconger.

Buoys and beacons

N Bartholomew
Red can buoy. Fl.R.5s.

Porth Conger Jetty
Beacon. ⚓ topmark. Q.G.

Leading marks

Line P
A back bearing of St Martin's daymark in line with summit of Creeb (041°) clears W of St Mary's

Directions

The approach to St Mary's Pool (see page 29) should be reversed to the point where Line C crosses Line P (⊕12), about 0.4M W of Steval (W extremity of St Mary's). From here a course of 192° should be steered towards St Agnes old lighthouse until about 300m N of Kallimay Point, St Agnes to clear Perconger Ledge and Little Perconger. Enter Porth Conger on a course of about 150°. At close to HW Hakestone (2m) may be seen above the bar between St Agnes and Gugh and this in line with the centre of the bar will assist in the line of approach . Local boatmen in their shallow draft vessels take a more direct route, passing close to Steval, just W of N Bartholomew and enter Porth Conger between The Cow and Tol Tuppens at the NW end of Gugh. The two chimneys of the Turks Head in transit clear The Calf (dries 3m) but this approach is not recommended without local knowledge.

The new quay at Porth Conger at LW showing The Cow and The Calf

Cow   Calf

St Agnes from N showing The Cow and Porth Conger in foreground and The Cove beyond
Patrick Roach

MAIN ANCHORAGES AND MOORINGS

The Cove (St Agnes and Gugh)

Sheltered SW-W-NW-N-NE-E. There is a good anchorage on sand towards the head of The Cove and good, deeper water, about half way up in about 7m. There is usually plenty of room and 20 yachts should present no problems. When the bar covers at HW quite a strong set develops to the SE. At this time it is dangerous to bathe on the bar. Otherwise the bathing is excellent. The Cove is probably the easiest of the southern anchorages to enter when arriving in Scilly from this direction. Just as the approach is relatively straightforward it is also a good departure anchorage (particularly to the S or E) at night, or preferably first light providing a safe exit bearing has been taken before sundown.

Porth Conger (St Agnes and Gugh)

Sheltered in winds from NE-E-SE-S-SW. This anchorage is situated on the other side of the bar which separates Gugh and St Agnes. This anchorage is not particularly recommended because there are permanent private moorings, little space for visitors and the holding is not very good. However, the anchorage is quite pretty and there is a good beach. There is a recently extended and improved landing quay with beacon and green ▲ topmark (Q.G), used by many ferries in the season and a lot of visitors. Enter on a SE heading between The Cow and St Agnes and anchor when the hill called Kittern on Gugh bears E. Depth 2m or less.

Porth Conger from Gugh with the Turk's Head and old lighthouse, St Agnes
Mike Lewin-Harris

MINOR ANCHORAGES

Dropnose Porth (Gugh)

49°53'.60N 06°19'.55W

Sheltered S-SW-W-NW. A shallow, rather open anchorage to E of Gugh with a very difficult approach and entrance. Should not be attempted without local knowledge.

Porth Killier (St Agnes)

49°53'.75N 06°20'.62W

A drying anchorage with a narrow entrance and two rocks in the centre. For use with care in settled weather only. The bottom is rocky with sand patches in places. Usually deserted.

Porth Coose (St Agnes)

49°53'.80N 06°21'.16W

Sheltered NE-E-SE-S-SW. An anchorage in 1.5m on sand and rock that requires great care in the approach and entrance. Subject to swell and should only be used in settled weather. Enter on a SW heading to Little Smith and S of Great Smith and Halftide Ledges. When the old lighthouse bears SE turn to port and enter. Normally deserted.

Periglis (St Agnes)

49°53'.60N 06°21'.00W

Sheltered N-NE-E-SE-S-SW-W. A drying anchorage for use with care. Enter on an E heading 50m to N of Penny Ledges and anchor near, but clear of, the permanent moorings. Two broken slips on the shore shaped like an inverted 'Y' for use by dinghies in calm weather. An alternative approach is with a white painted rock lying between the two arms of the 'Y' in line with the NW corner of the disused lifeboat house. A few visitors. Services are still conducted in the parish church nearby.

Little Porth Warna, Great Porth Warna, Little Porth Askin and Porth Askin (St Agnes)

49°53'.20N 06°20.75W

Sheltered WNW-N-NE-E-SE. A series of small coves where it is possible to anchor in settled weather but which have a difficult approach and there are many rocks near the anchorages. Enter on an E heading passing 200m to S of Long Point and just N of Western Rock. Anchor in 2m on sand and rock. Beware of the isolated rock, awash in the centre of St Warna's cove.

Dropnose Porth, Gugh, looking NE to Peninnis Head, St Mary's

Porth Killier, St Agnes

Porth Coose, St Agnes, looking NW with Tins Walbert daymark (left)

Periglis, St Agnes, with Burnt Island and Tins Walbert daymark

FACILITIES

Landing places

On the bar at The Cove and on the beach below the Turk's Head at Porth Conger but keep clear of the jetty.

Refuse

Large white bin (unmarked) on right at the top of the path from the beach – just before the road.

WCs

Public toilets by jetty in Porth Conger.

Telephones

Payphone at Turk's Head. Call box between Higher Town and Middle Town.

Internet

Wi-Fi at the Turk's Head, St Agnes.

Post Office and Shop

Near Middle Town (☎ 01720 423244). The PO offers currency exchange for French visitors, cheque encashment, Girobank, poste restante, faxes sent or received. The shop has a range of provisions including frozen and vegetarian food, wines, postcards, guide books, occasionally bread (may be reserved by 'phone/fax)

Eating out

Turk's Head Pub, Porth Conger (☎ 01720 422434). Covean Cottage (licenced) and Rose Cottage in Higher Town.

Ferries

From Porth Conger quay. Regular services to St Mary's in season as well as trips to other islands.

Church

C of E at Lower Town, above Periglis.

HISTORY AND VISITS ASHORE

St Agnes and Gugh

It is easy to walk around Gugh in an hour and worthwhile for the panoramic views and the sense of antiquity and remoteness. There are several prehistoric remains which are not always obvious amongst the heather. The most notable are Obadiah's Barrow, a stone tomb from the Bronze Age, and a 3m standing stone or monolith, known as the Old Man of Gugh. In early summer gulls nest along the shore, apparently oblivious to the gaze of humans.

After the ruggedness of Gugh, St Agnes seems relatively civilised with its neat cottages in the three settlements of Higher, Middle and Lower Towns and a chequerboard of flower fields protected by high hedges of pittosporum, hebe and tamarisk. The flower farms are concentrated around the disused lighthouse, one of the oldest in Britain. This was built in 1680 but was eventually superseded by the Bishop Rock lighthouse beyond the Western Rocks (see page 14) and subsequently by the Peninnis light on St Mary's in 1911. The structure on St Agnes is now kept whitewashed as a day mark; a most important one given its position.

In the days when St Agnes light was fuelled by coal it was sometimes alleged that the fire was deliberately neglected in order to mislead ships and attract lucrative wrecks. The power to attract ships was also attributed to St Warna, an Irish saint who, according to legend, landed at the cove of the same name. Perhaps it is not

Sundial on Gugh with the Turk's Head and slipway at Porth Conger, St Agnes beyond

surprising that the people of St Agnes were known as 'Turks' and were supposedly of swarthy appearance through interbreeding with foreign sailors. Whatever their reputation, the men were unrivalled throughout Scilly for their pilotage skills.

A concrete road, completed by the islanders themselves in the 1960s, leads to Periglis on the NW coast. The nineteenth-century church here was built on the site of an earlier one that had been funded from the proceeds of salvage. The name Periglis may be derived from the Celtic words for church and port, indeed the bay – a drying harbour – is used by local boats. The former lifeboat house stands at the top of the slipway. It was closed in 1920 but remains a testament to the many rescues organised from this strategically placed island at the SW extremity of Britain.

St Agnes and Gugh have always been isolated, even from the rest of the Isles of Scilly. In the distant past the northern islands formed a single land mass before it was 'drowned' by the sea and assumed its present form in about 700 AD while St Agnes, Gugh and Annet remained separate. The 12th century name for St Agnes seems to support this theory: it was Hagenes which may be translated as 'apart island'.

Annet and the Western Rocks

Among the numerous shipwrecks in the area, the worst recorded disaster happened in 1707 when a British fleet, under the command of Sir Cloudesley Shovell, was returning from the siege of Toulon. Owing to a miscalculation of longitude the fleet found itself not off Ushant but off Scilly and the flagship *Association* struck the Gilstone. Three other ships sank and over 1,600 men were lost. The body of the Admiral was washed ashore on the SE coast of St Mary's and he was subsequently given a state funeral.

In 1875 the Retarrier Ledges claimed the most serious wreck of the nineteenth century, the German transatlantic mail-steamer *Schiller* which was one of the largest vessels of her day. In dense fog she passed inside Bishop Rock and came to a violent stop. Only two lifeboats were successfully launched from the stricken ship and, out of a total compliment of 372 people on board there were just 37 survivors. Another casualty of huge size was the seven-masted schooner *Thomas W. Lawson*, the biggest sailing ship ever built. En route from Philadelphia to London in 1907, she was driven onto the Outer Ranneys, W of Annet, and broke up, shedding her cargo of crude oil. Sixteen of the eighteen crew died together with the St Agnes pilot who had gone to help. The lighthouse on Bishop Rock was already in operation when these tragedies occurred, having first been lit in 1858. Situated on a small ridge of rock that rises sheer from the depths, the

The Old Man
of Gugh

original iron structure was started in 1847 but swept away in a storm in 1850. It was replaced by a tower built of granite which was quarried in Cornwall, dressed on Rat Island, St Mary's and then shipped to the site. During the six years it took to complete the lighthouse the workers lived in huts on Rosevear and even managed to grow their own vegetables. In the 1880s the tower was reinforced and the height increased to 44m, making it the tallest lighthouse in the British Isles. A new light was also installed which could – and still can – be seen from 20 miles away.

Colonies of seabirds inhabit the islands; Annet is a sanctuary for puffins as well as the elusive storm petrel and Manx shearwater, and is closed to visitors between 15th April and 20th August. Grey seals also breed in the area, particularly on the Western Rocks. These rocks are 'the most wave-exposed found in England and Wales and are therefore considered to be of national importance', being designated a Special Area within the Isles of Scilly Marine Park.

5. FLORA, FAUNA, ARCHAEOLOGICAL

Birds

The Isles of Scilly have long been regarded as one of the best bird-watching regions in Britain. Although only about 50 species of birds actually breed on the islands, a wide range of migrants arrive during spring and autumn. This results in an annual total of usually about 240 species and a grand total, since records began in the nineteenth century, of over 400 different species. Moreover, many of the species on the British list were first sighted in Scilly and, in some cases, have only ever been seen there.

Seabirds account for a large proportion of the species that breed on Scilly. These include puffins on Annet, which is one of the southernmost breeding colonies, and Mincarlo. Although numbers decreased dramatically in the last century they are now on the increase and can be seen between April and September. Guillemots and razorbills are seen on the outer islands and, in the summer months, terns in the low-lying areas. Razorbills and terns are often found fishing between the islands, while guillemots and puffins go further afield for their catch. Waders, on their way to and from breeding grounds further north, use the smaller rocks for roosting.

Shags far outnumber cormorants in the islands, sometimes gathering in huge flocks to follow a school of fish. In winter, the great northern diver can be seen in more sheltered waters. In summer, both the Manx shearwater

A Bryher thrush
Mike Lewin-Harris

and the storm petrel may be sighted offshore, with the chance of some rarer shearwaters and petrels appearing in early autumn. Gannets are present throughout the year, and in larger numbers in the autumn, when the great and Arctic skuas are occasional visitors.

The islands have become wooded only in the last hundred years or so, consequently few woodland birds have reached Scilly. Woodpeckers are very rare, as are owls, treecreepers, jays and magpies, most having been recorded less than ten times. On the other hand, some birds have benefited from the hedges surrounding the flower fields, resulting in one of the highest concentrations of wren and song thrush in Britain, with robin, dunnock and blackbird not far behind. It will come as a surprise to most visitors that many of these birds are much less timid than their mainland counterparts.

Since most species are migrants, they can appear in unexpected places and it is not unusual to find land birds along the shore or waders foraging in the fields. However, there are favoured sites for certain species on each island. On St Mary's, there are two nature trails from the Lower and Higher Moors to Porth Hellick, which lead through marshes and past small pools; here swallows and martins are often observed, while warblers frequent the shallows and reeds nearby. The beaches around Hugh Town are excellent for shore birds, with turnstone, sanderling and oystercatcher in evidence most months, except during midsummer. The stonechat and rock pipit populate the strand line all year and are joined after the breeding season by the black redstart, chiffchaff and pied wagtail. The headlands around the island echo to the familiar call of the cuckoo, from late April until the end of June.

With the two largest lakes in Scilly and a substantial wooded area, Tresco is a unique island. The lakes attract a wide range of waterfowl during the winter months and have small breeding populations of tufted duck and gadwall. Herons are to be seen on the shore and beside the lakes and, in recent years, the number of egrets has increased greatly whilst the spoonbill is an occasional visitor. The surrounding trees and bushes are favoured by migrant flycatchers, warblers and other woodland birds, including such unusual species as golden oriole in the spring and yellow-browed warbler and red-breasted flycatcher in the autumn. In complete contrast is the rugged marine heath of Castle Down, in the N of Tresco, where wheatears, larks and pipits abound.

St Agnes is the most exposed of the major islands, bearing as it does the brunt of the SW winds, and its small patchwork fields with their tall hedges are a haven for tired migrants. Over the years, many very rare birds have stopped on this tiny island and more American vagrants have been recorded here than anywhere else in the UK. The beaches around the pool are among the best places in Scilly for observing waders, with redshank, greenshank, grey plover and purple sandpiper besides the more common species. In autumn, if the water level drops enough to expose some mud, the pool is also a good area for freshwater waders. The nearby cricket pitch is frequented by linnets, wheatears, pipits and the occasional rarity such as the short-toed lark or the hoopoe. In the S and W of the island, the open headlands have yet another range of birds: whimbrels are often seen on the short heather during the spring migration and sometimes, if the winds are in the W in the autumn, dotterels and American waders.

Because of its shape, the long, thin island of St Martin's produces an updraught, which is favoured by birds of prey and by the one pair of ravens known to be resident. Although the kestrel is the only bird of prey to breed regularly, peregrine, sparrowhawk and merlin are noted most months outside the breeding season, with harriers and kites recorded regularly. Chapel Down, on the E end of the island, has a small colony of breeding fulmars and some of the larger gulls breeding close by. The heathland here often yields the first Lapland and snow buntings of the autumn in September. In early summer, the northern slopes of the island are a haunt of cuckoos and stonechats, while in autumn many pipits and skylarks populate The Plains, where they may be disturbed by a passing kestrel or merlin. On the S side, the flower fields attract a great variety of migrants. The elms near the cricket pitch at Higher Town are a good site for insect-eating birds, such as warblers and flycatchers. Finally, the sand flats S of Middle Town can hold huge numbers of ringed plovers and sanderlings, especially in winter.

Bryher, with its spectacular views, offers the least shelter on the islands for foraging birds, but it still has much of interest. The open heaths, for instance, are popular with migrant ring ouzels. Any sunny hedge is worth watching for insect-catching birds and Bryher seems to do particularly well for the scarce icterine and melodious warblers during August and September. The neighbouring island of Samson has a large colony of lesser black-backed gulls and a small colony of kittiwakes nesting on the low cliffs. The sandy areas to the W are good spots to look for curlew, redshank, greenshank and the odd godwit.

Amateur or expert, the visitor who is interested in birds can find much to enjoy in Scilly.

Animals

Although the islands do not have many resident animals, they do boast one of the rarest in Britain. This is the lesser white-toothed shrew, known locally as the Scilly shrew, a tiny creature which is found throughout Scilly, but can be very difficult to spot.

The Atlantic grey seal breeds on the smaller outer rocks during the early autumn, when the pups may occasionally be seen, and is also present on the Eastern Isles.

Brown rats, rabbits and house and field mice inhabit all the major islands. Frogs are on St

Oystercatchers
Mike Lewin-Harris

Seals on the Western Rocks
Mike Lewin-Harris

Martin's and St Mary's, and slow worms have recently been released on Bryher. Hedgehogs have been introduced on St Mary's in the last twenty years and pipistrelle bats still survive in small numbers on the inhabited islands. At sea, harbour porpoise, several species of dolphin and the occasional whale are recorded most years, as well as basking shark.

Only a small number of butterflies breed on Scilly. Some of these, such as the meadow brown, common blue and speckled wood, have developed distinct sub-species on the islands. Migrant species like the red admiral and small tortoiseshell appear in huge numbers in some years, with the clouded yellow and painted lady being less common but also prone to having 'boom' years. Other migrant insects include some dragonflies, of which migrant hawkers are the most numerous, to such an extent that they may now be breeding. Among resident insects are common darters and some damselflies.

Flowers

The flora of the islands is very varied, with a range of habitats including coast and heath, hedgerow, ditch and marsh, stone walls, fields and waste ground. Many of the plants on Scilly are common in Cornwall and SW Britain, but there are several that are unknown on the mainland. A large number of plants are escapes from cultivation, mostly aliens from the Mediterranean, South Africa and South America, which may have been introduced through shipping, while others are former commercial crops that have become naturalized.

A few species occur on the islands right on the edge of their range. The dwarf pansy, for instance, is known in the UK only from Scilly and the Channel Islands, the nearest colonies being on the Atlantic seaboard of southern France. The flower-farming system means that

Nerine lillies in profusion – Tresco

the fields are left alone for most of the spring and this encourages wildflowers to grow in profusion. Thus, the Bermuda buttercup turns the fields yellow during late April and early May, while the ubiquitous three-cornered leek invades almost every garden.

Most of the windbreak hedges originate from the southern hemisphere, notably the New Zealand pittosporum, which is the most efficient. Coprosma, olearia and hebe, from the same country, are also used, together with euonymus from Japan and escallonia from Chile. The commonest deciduous tree is the native British elm, which has so far escaped the destructive Dutch elm disease. Shelter belts of Monterey and lodge pole pines criss-cross many of the islands, although the former are being replaced because they are less resilient to winter gales.

A walk along the cliffs in early summer will reveal masses of thrift, birdsfoot trefoil, English stonecrop and foxgloves; like many red or pink-flowered plants on Scilly, the foxglove is usually a much darker colour than its mainland counterpart. The Hottentot fig or ice plant, from South Africa, carpets large areas. It belongs to the mesembryanthemum family, of which several members are now regarded as naturalized on the islands.

Scilly is always associated with the daffodil, which is grown as a commercial crop. Many varieties of daffodil and Tazetta narcissus have escaped from the fields and grow wild in the hedgerows, where they tend to flower in early spring after the peak of the winter picking season. Other commercial escapes include iris and whistling jacks (a purple gladiolus) flowering in early summer, followed by agapanthus and amaryllis in late summer.

Basic checklists for the birds and flowers of Scilly can be obtained from the tourist office or Isles of Scilly Wildlife Trust, Hugh Town, St Mary's (see opposite).

Tresco Abbey Gardens

Once described as 'Kew Gardens with the lid off', Tresco Abbey Gardens contain a range of exotic plants that is unrivalled in the British Isles, if not the world. Thanks to the unique climatic conditions of Tresco, the gardens are very rarely affected by temperatures below freezing; at the same time, they benefit from warm air currents produced by the Gulf Stream and from constant high humidity created by the sea. Shelter, however, is the final essential ingredient and, for this reason, the gardens are surrounded by windbreaks to protect them from the savage, salt-laden gales of winter. All these factors enable an extraordinary collection of plants to flourish.

To visit Tresco Abbey Gardens is to visit not one garden but many. South Africa, Australia, New Zealand, South America, Mexico, California, the Canary Islands and Madeira are but a few of the regions represented by the plants growing here, with the emphasis on the southern hemisphere. The gardens extend to an area of little over 20 acres and are arranged in a series of S-facing terraces on a gentle slope, protected to the N and W by hillsides covered in conifers and evergreens.

The Top Terrace looks out over the sea towards St Agnes and St Mary's. Although exposed to the salt winds, its sun-baked soil is an ideal home for South African plants and notably for the spectacular, summer-flowering proteas (this being the most northerly place in the world where they grow outside). Descending to the Middle Terrace, through 40ft high Canary Island palms, one could easily imagine oneself in the Mediterranean. The outstanding feature, from spring onwards, is the tree echiums; also from the Canaries, these relatives of our native viper's bugloss send up tall, rocket-like spires of deep blue flowers, with variations in pink or almost red. Blue agapanthus have seeded themselves in rocky corners and succulents from many countries cling to the granite cliffs. This part of the gardens also suits the puyas which, like pineapple, belong to the bromeliad family; their huge, prickly spikes of yellow or metallic blue flowers appear in early summer and are pollinated by blackbirds on Tresco, in the absence of the hummingbirds of their native Chile.

There is very much more to see within these exciting and varied gardens. From early spring to late autumn, the visitors will be rewarded with a wealth of colour and interest and an unforgettable experience.

)01720 424105
www.tresco.co.uk

Tresco Abbey Gardens *Mike Lewin-Harris*

The Isles of Scilly Wildlife Trust

The Trust cares for the wildlife sites that make up 60% of the landmass of Scilly. The Trust is also concerned with what goes on under the water and on the islands' shores. The Isles of Scilly Marine Biodiversity Project has been set up to learn more about the rich marine habitats and species of the Isles of Scilly.

)01720 422153
www.ios-wildlifetrust.org.uk

Area of Outstanding Natural Beauty

In 1976 the Isles of Scilly were designated an Area of Outstanding Natural Beauty and the primary purpose is to 'conserve and enhance the natural beauty of the landscape'. A partnership of organisations work together in Scilly through an AONB advisory committee to ensure that all parties in the islands cooperate in using their powers for the long term benefit of the Isles of Scilly AONB.

www.ios-aonb.info

INDEX